Jesse Milton Emerson

New York to the Orient

A Series of Letters Written during a Brief Trip Through Europe to Palestine,

Returning via Egypt, Italy, France, and England. Third Edition

Jesse Milton Emerson

New York to the Orient
A Series of Letters Written during a Brief Trip Through Europe to Palestine, Returning via Egypt, Italy, France, and England. Third Edition

ISBN/EAN: 9783337149130

Printed in Europe, USA, Canada, Australia, Japan

Cover: Foto ©Andreas Hilbeck / pixelio.de

More available books at **www.hansebooks.com**

NEW YORK TO THE ORIENT.

A SERIES OF LETTERS WRITTEN DURING A BRIEF TRIP THROUGH EUROPE TO PALESTINE, RETURNING VIA EGYPT, ITALY, FRANCE, AND ENGLAND.

WITH A

DESCRIPTION OF THE WRITER'S EXPERIENCE ON THE STEAMSHIP *OREGON* AT THE TIME OF HER LOSS.

BY

J. M. EMERSON.

THIRD EDITION.

NEW YORK:
E. R. PELTON & CO.
1887.

PREFACE.

THESE letters were originally addressed to the readers of the *Yonkers Gazette*, at the request of many of whom they now appear in book form.

If that portion of the public whom they may chance to reach find them as worthy of approval, and judge them as leniently as did those to whom they were originally addressed, the author will only feel that he has widened his circle of indulgent friends.

J. M. E.

NEW YORK, September, 1886.

CONTENTS.

LETTER I.
                                                                                 PAGE

Taking Passage for Europe—Less Risk in the Voyage than in the Daily Use of a Horse and Carriage—A Storm at Sea—Bad Cooking on Ocean Steamers—The City of London—Its Immensity—Old-Fogyism there—Large Addition to the Voting Classes, etc., etc.................... 11

LETTER II.

London to Paris—The Mann Boudoir-Cars—An Amusing Incident—Hôtel la Grand de Russe—The College at Varna—Pluck and Bravery of the Bulgarians—Arrival at Constantinople—Turkish Baths there and in America—Stamboul and its Mosques—Wonderful Stories about them—The Call to Prayer—A Grand Bazaar—Other Points of Interest—A Visit to the Whirling Dervishes—The Turk Chronically Opposed to all Improvements—Interesting Anecdotes—Dearth of News.............. 19

LETTER III.

Leaving Constantinople - Observing Thanksgiving Day—The Excellent Defences of Constantinople—Arrival at Smyrna—One of the Oldest Cities of the World—A Description Thereof—The Bazaar and Its Peculiarities—The Turk's Creed—Display of Brigands' Heads—The Island of Chios—The Effect of Earthquakes—Samos, Patmos, and Rhodes—Then Direct for Cyprus—Beyrout—The American Presbyterian Mission there—Off for Baalbec by Diligence—An irrepressible Chicago Yankee—Ascending the Lebanon Mountains and on to Damascus—The Manufacture of Silk—The Ruins of Baalbec—Mt. Hermon in the Distance.. 37

LETTER IV.

The Earliest Records of Baalbec—Something about its Ruins—The Great Temple of the Sun, with a Description of its Ruins—Most of the Holy Places Mythical—A Mingling of Ancient and Modern Work—A Smaller Temple also Dedicated to the Sun—The Journey to Damascus Resumed.. 51

LETTER V.

Back to Shtora—By Diligence to Damascus—Its Famed Gardens—A Cool Reception, but a Fire and Good Dinner Warm us—The Oldest City in Palestine—Its Celebrated Blades and Silk Manufactures—All Labor-Saving Machinery Resisted—The Mosques—Head of John the Baptist—The Great Bazaar—The " East Gate of the City "—House of Ananias—Paul's Prison—The Private Houses—Witnessing the Rite of Circumcision—The House of Naaman—Massacre of 1860—It was Encouraged by the Turkish Government—An Interesting Episode 59

LETTER VI.

Jaffa, the Joppa of Scripture—The House of Simon, the Tanner—Off for Jerusalem—Something about Ramleh—The Church of the Nativity at Bethlehem, and the Christmas Celebration thereat ; the Legends connected therewith—The Plain of Bethlehem—The Field of Boaz—Jerusalem, City of the Great King—What was Seen on a Tour through it—A Few Words about the American Consul 71

LETTER VII.

Further Descriptions in and about Jerusalem—Solomon's Temple—Mosque of Omar—The Holy Rock where Abraham Offered up Isaac—Mosque of El Aksa—Christ's Cradle—Church of the Sepulchre—Warring Sects—The Hill of Calvary—Other Sacred Spots and Relics—Remarkable Ruins—Church of St. Ann—Pool of Bethesda—Tombs of the Kings—The Brook Kedron—Mount of Olives—Pool of Siloam and other Sacred Places—The German Colony—Back to Jaffa 80

LETTER VIII.

From Haifa to Nazareth—First View of the City—At the Latin Convent and Monastery—The House and Kitchen of the Virgin—Church of the Annunciation—A Lesson for Christians of Europe and America—Old Greek Church—The Well of Mary—Orphan Asylum for Girls—Back to the Dirty City—Among the Native Artisans—An Arab Wedding—Cana of Galilee—The New Church there 91

LETTER IX.

A Visit to Mount Carmel—The Cave of Elijah—Site of the Ancient City of Sycaminum—Rock Caves—Carmelite Monastery—The Mahkraka—Hill of the Priests—A Sacred Grove—A Legend Thereof—At the Druse Village of Dalieh—Some of their Customs—A Primitive Method of Divorce—Ruins of Thirty Cities in Mount Carmel—Honeycombed with Tombs, etc 100

Contents.

LETTER X.

Haifa and Acre—Delightful Winter Weather—Cheap Fruit—The Olive Crop—The Features of Haifa—Enterprise of its German Colony—Their Persecutions—Monumental Manure-Heaps—Acre, One of the Oldest Cities in the World—Besieged Seventeen Times—The Rivers Kishon and Belus—Discovery of Glass—Jezzar, the Butcher Pasha of Acre, etc., etc.. 110

LETTER XI.

Leaving Haifa—Homeward Bound—Stopping on the Way—At Port Said—Poor Steamers and Worse Accommodations—Ismailia—An Old and Handsomely Laid Out Town—Cairo, the Largest City in Africa—Street Scenes—The Khedive's and Other Official Residences—The Pyramids of Gizeh—Road Leading Thereto—The Great Pyramid of Cheops—The Sphinx—Old Cairo—Church of St. Mary—The Most Ancient Mosque in Egypt—The Island of Rhodda—Its Nileometer—The Citadel—Sapero Mosque—An Obelisk—Ostrich Farm—Chateau of Gezireh, etc., etc... 121

LETTER XII.

From Cairo to Alexandria—The Valley of the Nile—How the Land is Irrigated—Different Methods of Raising the Water—The Wonderful Land of Egypt—Alexandria—A Visit to Pompey's Pillar—The Catacombs—Leaving Alexandria—Review of, and Reflections upon, the Journey thus far—Valuable Things Learned about Business, Eating, etc.—Some Advice—Messina in Sicily.. 133

LETTER XIII.

Leaving Messina—The Volcano of Stromboli—Bay of Naples—How it Compares with New York Bay—The City of Naples—A Visit to Pompeii—Description of the Houses—The Temples, Theatres, and Basilicas—Herculaneum—The Museum and its Statuary from the Buried Cities—Palaces, Catacombs, and Tombs—A Ride through Naples—An Eruption of Mount Vesuvius........................... 143

LETTER XIV.

A Sight of Vesuvius in Eruption—Leaving Naples and the Journey to Rome—In the Holy City—A Visit to St. Peter's Church—Its Marvels—The Vatican, the Pope's Prison—Galleries of Pictures and Statuary—The Capitol Museum—Other Attractions, etc., etc..................... 154

Contents.

LETTER XV.

Yet Tarrying in Rome—More of the Sights of the Ancient City—Italy and America Wedded—Increase of Art Taste—The Colosseum—The Forum—Other Celebrated Structures—The Pantheon—The King's Residence—Castle of St. Angelo—Ruins of the Baths of Caracalla—The Catacombs, etc., etc.. 163

LETTER XVI.

Leaving Rome—A Country of many Railroad Tunnels—The Carrara Marble Quarries—Pisa and its Leaning Tower and other Attractions—Genoa, the Principal Seaport of Italy—Milan—"The Last Supper"—The Great Cathedral—Description thereof—View from its Tower—Leaving Milan—The Alps Scenery—Arrival at Basle.................. 171

LETTER XVII.

Palestine and Paris Contrasted—First Impression of the Latter City—An Art-Loving People—Moving the Statue of the Venus de Milo—A Contrast in Steps—The Hotels of Paris—The Restaurants—Wine Consumption—The French Great Lovers of Amusement—Grand Opera House—The Art-Galleries and their Treasures—Various Points of Interest... 179

LETTER XVIII.

Paris to London—Poor Railway Accommodations—Old London—Devastated by Fires, Pestilences, and Civil Wars—The Original City One Square Mile—Fragments of the Old Wall still Standing—Official Integrity—No Broadway Railroad Steal Possible here—Adhering to Old Methods—National Conceit—Antiquated Railroad Methods—Expressage Peculiarities—Underground, Surface, and Elevated or Upper Level Railroads—Ancient Guilds—Home Rule for Ireland—A London Banquet.. 192

LETTER XIX.

Leaving London for New York—Homeward Bound on the Ill-fated *Oregon*—A Faithful, Accurate, and Graphic Description of the Fearful Disaster—Behavior of the Officers and Crew—Heroism of the Passengers—On the Verge of Eternity—A Fortunate Escape—The Combination of Favorable Circumstances which Resulted in the Saving of Every Soul on Board... 203

NEW YORK TO THE ORIENT.

LETTER I.

Taking Passage for Europe—Less Risk in the Voyage than in the Daily Use of a Horse and Carriage—A Storm at Sea—Bad Cooking on Ocean Steamers—The City of London—Its Immensity—Old-Fogyism there—Large Addition to the Voting Classes, etc., etc.

LONDON, December 3, 1885.

IN complying with the request to embody in some letters for publication the observation and experiences of a journey to the Orient, I wish to request my readers to anticipate only such a result as they might naturally expect from the use of a very moderate amateur ability in that line. Such a trip can hardly fail to furnish the requisite material for this purpose, as it will embrace not only Palestine but something of Egypt and the various European countries: England, France, Italy, Turkey, etc.

I take passage in the *Gallia*, of the Cunard line. The choice among the different lines had been to some extent influenced by a former experience of the great care and watchfulness exercised in the management of their vessels, as well as by the claim they make that they have never lost the life of a passenger in an experience of over forty years, since the line was established. This is certainly a most remarkable record, and serves forcibly to illustrate the very small percentage of risk attending a voyage to Europe. There is much less risk than in the daily use of a horse and carriage. For in the latter case one is subject to constant danger from the caprices of a freaky animal, while the forces which propel the steamer, and the appliances which control the elements, are much more subject to human control.

The experiences of a voyage at sea are so monotonous that it would take the pen of a Dickens to make a detailed account of it interesting, hence I shall naturally pass it lightly. The hour of departure was so early—6 A.M.—that most of the passengers slept on board the previous night—an experience they will be little likely to repeat, as the discomforts of the close state-room are even greater than when at sea, and one is wise to avoid adding a single night to the number necessarily involved in making the voyage. In consequence of the early hour there was less of bustle and confusion than usually accompanies the departure of an European passenger-steamer.

Promptly at the hour the enormous vessel swings out into the stream, accompanied by two other large steamships going in the same direction. But we part company with them in a few hours and see them no more. For three days we have a smooth sea, and most of the passengers are promptly on hand at meals, and all are promising themselves a smooth passage. On the fourth morning we find a "fence" erected around the dishes on the table, and very few people appear in their seats to make the attempt to climb the fence in search of their breakfast. Mysterious sounds of distress now reach the ear from the state-rooms, while a few more adventurous individuals are on deck leaning over the rail, each contributing his little quota to swell the volume of the briny deep. The courage of the previous three days is at a large discount. But the few who are in a condition to enjoy it are treated to one of the grandest of all sights—a storm at sea. Such a storm has burst upon us with tremendous fury. The great ship, a ponderous mass that it would seem no earthly power could move when lying at the wharf, now tosses like a frail bark upon the mighty waves. Such a storm furnishes a wonderful illustration of the Almighty power; and such perfect command of the vessel all through the storm shows most vividly the control that man has acquired over the elements.

The passengers, rather few in numbers—only about fifty—at first seem reserved and distant in their bearing towards each other, but every evening they mingle together like members of one family, and when they arrive in Liverpool they part like old friends.

A word about the *cuisine* of the steamship. I have often crossed the Atlantic in the steamers of different lines, and have always found the cooking gross and uninviting. All the meats, and in fact all dishes, are cooked beforehand and are generally overdone and greasy, and thus indigestible for the delicate stomach. There is a great abundance, and an immense amount of food is wasted. If some one of the prominent lines would inaugurate the plan of charging a fixed sum for the passage, and serve meals on the restaurant plan, allowing each passenger to pay for just what he orders, and have the dishes cooked as ordered, I am sure it would be a pronounced success. There is no reason why one should not have the best of cooking on an ocean steamer as well as in a first-class hotel.

If the above plan should not be deemed practicable, there surely is no good cause why a steamer should not employ an experienced *chef*, and have the meals cooked to order, as in all our best hotels. There is no lack of time, for the passengers have the entire day on hand and never need hurry at meals. The complaint of the grossness and unskilfulness in the cooking and serving meals on all the Atlantic lines is so general that it seems strange that some enterprising company does not take the lead in this matter and inaugurate a reform. I know that many persons would give such a line the preference.

The *Gallia*, being now an old steamer, is quite slow as compared with the larger and more modern ships of the same line. We are nine and a half days from New York to Liverpool. A night at Liverpool and a five-hours' ride on the Midland Railway through, among other shires, the very picturesque county of Derby, brings us to London, where we propose to enjoy a brief rest.

This city is increasing in population with great rapidity, something like two hundred thousand each year, and is said to number now nearly five million souls. This huge population is scattered over an area of about two hundred and fifty square miles. One accustomed to other large cities can master the largest of them in a few days, but when he comes to London he finds it too much for him, within any reasonable period. He may think he knows London, and suddenly some day finds himself in the midst of a labyrinth of streets, and rows of buildings almost without end, which are all quite new to him. I have spent weeks in London and have often repeated this experience.

Every time I visit England I am reminded afresh of the exceedingly conservative spirit pervading the people. Not only is this true of the aristocratic classes, but of most of the men of influence who control large public institutions, railroads, insurance companies, banks, etc. The head of a department in one of the great railway companies here informed me that he demonstrated to the Board of Directors that, by adopting the use of condensed gas for lighting the cars of the road, they could save many thousand pounds annually, besides a great amount of labor and trouble. The board refused to make the change. This board was composed mainly of old men, one prominent member being eighty-five years old. The same is true of the system for checking the baggage of railroad passengers. The American system has been carefully examined and pronounced far superior to any system in vogue in Europe, and would seem to be admirably adapted to the roads of the United Kingdom, where there are so many branch roads, which makes it difficult for a passenger to keep trace of his baggage, and keeps him in a constant state of apprehension lest it shall get astray ; yet the directors of all the leading roads refuse to adopt it. A small commencement has, however, been made in this direction, as baggage can now be checked on this system from any hotel or private house in New York to any point in London or Liverpool for a charge of one dollar. It can also be checked, in the same way, from the landing wharves in Liverpool to London. This much has evidently been done at the demand of American passengers, who constitute a very large fraction of the ocean travel between the two countries, and it is quite possible that in the course of twenty-five or fifty years it will be generally adopted.

But, while we find some things like the above open to criticism, there are, on the other hand, many excellent things which we on the other side of the Atlantic might well adopt. But I hope to enter more fully into these matters in a future letter on returning from the long journey proposed.

The all-absorbing topic in England at this time is the addition of some 2,000,000 to the voters of the United Kingdom, mostly agricultural laborers, in conformity with a law recently enacted. This concession is said to have been unwillingly made by those holding the balance of power, under apprehension of coming trouble, and there can be but little doubt of the wisdom of the measure under the circumstances.

LETTER II.

London to Paris—The Manu Boudoir-Cars—An Amusing Incident—Hôtel la Grand de Russe—The College at Varna—Pluck and Bravery of the Bulgarians—Arrival at Constantinople—Turkish Baths there and in America—Stamboul and its Mosques—Wonderful Stories about them—The Call to Prayer—A Grand Bazaar—Other Points of Interest—A Visit to the Whirling Dervishes—The Turk Chronically Opposed to all Improvements—Interesting Anecdotes—Dearth of News.

CONSTANTINOPLE, Dec. 8, 1885.

ON arriving in London, and learning that quarantine, on account of the cholera, prevailed again in Italy and Egypt, I conclude to go by Constantinople and return by those countries. Leaving London in the morning by the express-train for Paris, and passing the Channel from Dover to Calais, which is always very disagreeable even in the most favorable weather, we have a five-hours' ride through a dismal country, with train accommodations as bad as possible, though we hold a first-class ticket. An American needs only to make this trip to feel a commendable pride in the railroad accommodations of his own country.

We arrive at Paris just in season to get din

ner and take the express-train for Constantinople at 7.30. This train is made up of Mann boudoir cars, with dining-car attached, and is run by a company which also runs a similar train over the other leading continental roads, charging the passengers about twenty per cent. more than the regular railroad fare for first-class tickets, in addition to a round sum for the sleeping cars. The meals are served at a fixed price, wines extra. This style of car, I understand, was originated in Chicago, and the inventor, Mr. Mann, came to Europe to introduce them, and, after making considerable progress in that direction, he sold out all his interests in Europe to the company which runs these express trains, for 1,000,000 francs, and returned to America to introduce them there. I rode in one of his cars last May from Detroit to Chicago. On the whole they are more convenient and comfortable than the Pullman Sleepers. There is a passage along one side of the car, and the other side is occupied by compartments for two or four passengers each. These small rooms afford more privacy and comfort than is possible in the Pullman cars, and the toilet-rooms are also more private and convenient. I did not expect, after former experiences in railroad travelling on the continent, to find such facilities and conveniences as are now attainable on several of the main routes through Europe.

As we stop only two, three, or five minutes even in the larger cities, such as Strasburg, Stuttgart, Munich, and Vienna, I do not step off the train till we reach the Danube crossing to Rustchuk—a distance of 2,300 miles. An amusing incident occurred during the examination of my baggage on the frontier of Hungary. The officer spied a big red apple which I had brought from America, and eagerly seized it. I protested, and demanded the reason of his action. He caught the meaning rather from my manner than from the words spoken, I have no doubt, for his knowledge of plain English was unquestionably limited, and exclaimed, "Phylloxera!" So I lost my beautiful apple, but I have no doubt my loss was his gain.

The time through from London to Constantinople—2,800 miles—is four days. We are compelled to spend one night at Varna, the end of our railroad ride, on account of the high sea, which renders it impossible to get the passengers and mails on board of the steamer lying in the bay some half a mile from the wharf. All passengers are taken off to the steamers in small boats, and all goods in barges. Having formed the acquaintance of a Queen's messenger, who was bearing dispatches to the British minister at Constantinople, we get a room together at the Hôtel la Grand de Russe. When we gain a full knowledge of the proportions and accommodations of the establishment we discover a singular appropriateness in not naming it Le Grand Hôtel de Russe. But the "grand" must come in somewhere.

Having called with my new acquaintance on the British Consul, and having received an invitation to lunch with him the following day, our enjoyment of the hospitality of the Hôtel la Grand de Russe is lessened to that extent, not specially to our regret, for we have an elaborate repast, savoring of the true English style of hospitality, and are afterwards accompanied by our host to the steamer.

There is a large college at Varna, numbering several hundred students and a large quota of professors. The war feeling is said to run high here, and the students and professors seem to be very patriotic, as nearly all the adults of the former, and all the latter except three, have volunteered for the war, and have already seen some hard fighting. It seems that on the breaking out of the war the Bulgarians had very few capable officers, and that not only the Servians confidently expected to achieve an easy victory over them, but the Russians, knowing their lack of officers, expected to be called upon to supply them, which would naturally assist that country in its designs upon Constantinople; and so there will be much bitter disappointment at the wonderful pluck and bravery of the Bulgarians.

At sunrise the next morning we arrive at the Bosphorus, which connects the Black Sea with the Sea of Marmora much in the same way as the East River connects Long Island Sound with New York harbor, and at 9 A.M. we arrive at Constantinople. Much of the distance from the Black Sea the shores of the Bosphorus are studded with the villas of Turkish officials, foreign ministers, consuls, etc., and the wealthy merchants of the great city, which they use for summer residences. On the confines of the city are several immense palaces, very elaborate and costly, belonging to the sultan, the principal ones of which are usually visited by travellers who remain long enough to compass the formalities necessary to gain admission, which must be done through the foreign minister for each nationality. The sultan keeps himself very secluded; is always surrounded by military guards, and is said to be in constant fear of assassination; and it is not unlikely his fears are well founded, for many of his predecessors have lost their lives in that manner.

After securing quarters at the Hôtel d'Angleterre, and engaging a dragoman—which functionary is very necessary, especially for a short visit—the first use I made of him was to conduct me to a Turkish bath. I found the bath very refreshing after the long railroad journey; but neither here nor in London did I find the Turkish bath so complete in all the appointments requisite for such an establishment, and especially of cleanliness, as is that of Dr. Shepard, on Brooklyn Heights, our own favorite bath for the past twenty years. The doctor is entitled to the distinction of being the pioneer in introducing the Turkish bath into America, after having first visited England, France, and Turkey, and gained knowledge of the best methods, etc., etc. The doctor is one of the few men who have become inspired with an idea, the working out of which he believes would serve to benefit humanity, and to make it his life-work to practically embody that idea.

Being refreshed by the bath and the first meal in Constantinople, which they call breakfast—

served at twelve o'clock—I took a carriage and my guide and proceeded to Stamboul, which is the distinctively Mohammedan quarter of the great city, and separated from the part more occupied by Christians by a long iron bridge, made in England and put up by English mechanics.

There are many very large mosques here, and we visited several of them, and especially the St. Sophia, which was built and long occupied by the Christians (as are many others here), but for several hundred years has been occupied and constantly used for purposes of worship by the Mohammedans. It is an exceedingly massive structure, some parts of the walls being evidently ten or twelve feet thick. It contains an immense amount of fine marble and mosaic work finished with great elaboration in detail.

The Mohammedans have effaced nearly all the emblems of the Christian faith, the cross, heads and faces of angels, saints, etc., which greatly disfigures the building. My guide gravely informed me that when the Mohammedans took possession of the building, on which occasion they slaughtered thousands of Christians who had gathered there for protection, two of the windows at the base of the dome were walled up with marble, by direct act of God, to show his displeasure—the guide, of course, is a Christian—and that when the Christians regain possession (which they all believe they are sure to do) these windows will be miraculously restored. He also informed me that, during that terrible massacre, a prominent Christian priest was directed by an angel to pass through a gate into a certain room, and he would be saved and the slaughter stopped. He entered the room, and the doors and windows were instantly walled up solid, and the lives of the people remaining in the church were saved. He added that the priest had been in this room six hundred years, and that he would come out alive when the church should be restored to the Christians. He asked me: "Don't you believe it?" On expressing a mild form of doubt as to a strictly literal interpretation and asking him: "Do you believe it?" he answered: "Yes, indeed, it is so; I know it."

That settled the matter, and we proceeded to further investigate the mysteries and wonders of the grand old buildings, and my guide had no lack of wonderful and miraculous things to relate. He showed me a very large marble pillar, surrounded at its base by a sheet of brass about a quarter of an inch thick. A hole had been worn through the brass and into the marble some three inches by the fingers of the faithful, who found water there, miraculously supplied, with which to cross themselves. The water ceased to flow when the Christians lost possession of the church, although faithful Mohammedans had ever since placed their fingers there and crossed themselves. But the water will flow again as soon as the Christians regain possession. As we passed through the mosque under the grand dome, many of the faithful were kneeling on the stone floor at their devotions, but I noticed that some of them paid more attention to us than to their prayers.

The Mohammedans have built their tall minarets upon the old buttresses laid by the Christians to support the church structure. They are of uniform shape, and many of them are very high. As we came out of the mosque it was the hour of sunset, and we heard the call to prayer from the gallery of one of the minarets far above our heads. The not unmusical voice, with the peculiar intoning, combined with the surrounding sights and sounds, produced a strange and weird effect.

The mosques are very numerous, and many of

them are large and massive. A majority of them have been built by the different sultans to perpetuate their name and reign. Each one also builds a tomb in which to be buried with his family, and a clock at the tomb for the faithful to regulate their watches by and leave their benediction. The clock is usually surrounded by a crowd of Mohammedans enjoying this privilege and performing their pious duty.

We next visited the Grand Bazaar, which covers many acres, and is said to be the largest bazaar in the world. It is quite imposing as a whole, but almost contemptible in detail, being composed mostly of small stalls or shops, filled with every kind of Turkish product, all made by hand, for there is no such thing as improvement here. One seems to be suddenly transported beyond the pale of civilization; no railroads, no machinery, no factories, no labor-saving appliances, everything just as it was hundreds of years ago, and that, too, in a great city of a million population. A good illustration of what I would like to convey is furnished by the fact that it will take me nearly as long to complete my journey from Constantinople to Haifa, a distance of about twelve hundred miles, as it has to come from New York to Constantinople, a distance of six thousand miles—viz., sixteen days. This is rather discouraging after congratulating myself on arriving here that my journey was nearly completed.

The architecture of the city, outside of the palaces of the sultan and the mosques, is by no means remarkable, although some of the legations have rather imposing buildings, notably the German and the English.

The streets are very narrow, and, between the hordes of dirty vagrant dogs and dirtier men and women, they present an appearance anything but inviting. The smells and the noises complete a picture more disgusting than is afforded by any city that it has ever been my fortune to visit.

Another special point of interest here is the old wall of the ancient city. We visited first the celebrated seven towers, which are on the side of the city washed by the Sea of Marmora. They are very high, wonderfully massive, and admirably adapted for defence. The old wall, with smaller towers at intervals of a few hundred yards, extends around the entire old city and had many gates. For centuries after the wall was built (over one thousand years ago) the gates were daily opened, closed, and guarded.

Now the gateways are used, but the gates are gone. The wall, with its towers and gateways and the three ditches outside, constitutes one of the most picturesque old ruins to be found in any quarter of the world. The ditches have been partially filled up and are rented by the city to gardeners, who raise vegetables for the city market.

On our return to the city outside the walls we make a visit to one of the churches of the dancing dervishes and witness one of their extraordinary performances. There are about forty of them, with a chief priest at their head, enclosed in a fenced space about thirty feet square, in the centre of the building. At first they all kneel in prayer upon the floor, which is polished smooth by the bare feet. After the prayer comes the music, singing, with flutes accompanying, also drums beating. Soon the whirling commences, all spinning around rapidly for some ten minutes; then they rest about two minutes and spin again for ten minutes more. The whole performance reminds one of the scenes that are sometimes enacted at Methodist camp-meetings, the advantage resting with the Methodist, because his enthusiasm is genuine—inspired from some source—while that of the dervishes appears to be perfunctory, the oft repeating of which tends to tameness and formality. The head priest of the order is married, and owns the church and a fine mansion, with extensive grounds, which all pass to his successor at his death, while the ordinary priests are not permitted to marry. They appear to lead a very easy, lazy life, their work consisting of the daily religious ceremonies, which are generally performed in private, the public being admitted only on Wednesdays.

In making these visits we ride many miles and pass through almost all parts of the city. We see some of the appliances of Western civilization, such as the tramway, the sewing-machine, etc., but they are brought here by Englishmen and Americans, quite against the protest of the Turk. He is chronically opposed to all improvements, as you would readily believe by witnessing the appliances and methods in daily use. I saw to-day a number of diminutive asses trudging along through the streets with very long pieces of lumber strapped to their backs. The same useful little animal constitutes himself a walking baking-shop, with two large baskets filled with bread strung over his back, each of which is larger than the animal himself.

I saw several groups of loaded camels passing through the streets with their ungainly forms and deliberate step; also, droves of sheep just arrived from Asia, with splendid coats of shining wool. These scenes, with an occasional European carriage, with the tramways running on several of the principal streets, with crowds of poverty-stricken refugees from the various surrounding countries entering the city, with the gypsies who live here in large numbers, with an immense number of Jews festering in their filth; with Armenians, Greeks, and Christians, and, above all, with the Mohammedans, the dominant race, standing doggedly in the way of all improvement, it is easy to understand why Constantinople is called the most cosmopolitan city in the world.

The Turk differs as much as possible from the Western races, not only in mental methods, but in his manners and habits of daily life. It is said that the difference between a Turk and a Christian, in Turkey, is that the Turk when he wishes to do you honor puts on his hat and takes off his boots, while the Christian puts on his boots and takes off his hat.

Contrary to the idea entertained usually in regard to the Turks, it is the universal testimony that the lower orders are reliable and honest, while the higher orders do not sustain so good a reputation in this respect. I heard many anecdotes illustrative of this point. A certain common Turk, connected with a steamer running between two cities, is often entrusted with large sums of money, in some cases thousands of pounds, and the delivery is always faithful and prompt. On one occasion he had £3,000 strapped around his person. The steamer was lost in a storm and the boats smashed, and he was most roughly handled. But he delivered the money, while many a Christian would have kept it and sworn it was lost.

Another incident is told of Mustapha, a common Turk, who belongs to a life-saving corps, organized after the plan of ours in America. On one occasion, when a ship was wrecked off a high bluff, in the night, they could hear the cries of distress under the bluff. Mustapha was let down the bluff one hundred feet by a rope secured around his body. He found a seaman struggling with the waves dashing against the bluff. He seized him and was himself dashed senseless by the waves and lost his man. But he was drawn up, and soon, on recovering consciousness, he went down again in the same manner, with the same result. He was let down the third time and brought up the sailor, or rather his body, for he was now dead. Was not Mustapha a better Christian than the man who believes in "salvation by faith," and refuses to risk his own life to save that of his brother?

The Turks, even of the lower order, do not become servants to the people of other nationalities, and in most cases where they are servants to the higher classes of their own race they are slaves. Most of the women of the harems are slaves.

The city is divided nearly in the middle by the Golden Horn, and the situation reminds one forcibly of New York and its surroundings. Stamboul, situated on a peninsula, represents New York City. The other part of the city, which is called Pera, represents Brooklyn, while Scutari, across the wide river, with the immense structure established by Florence Nightingale as an hospital in the late war in plain sight, represents Jersey City. New York, Naples, and Constantinople are said to possess the most beautiful harbors in the world. I have not yet seen the bay of Naples, but to my eye the bay of New York is finer than that of Constantinople.

It seems very strange to an American, who

reads in his morning paper the news from all parts of the world, that here he must go weeks and weeks without news from anywhere, so absolute is the censorship of the press. We learn nothing here in Constantinople of the proceedings of the great conference now being held here. It is scarcely alluded to in the papers, and news of its doings reaches this city in the English papers, printed some three thousand miles away. The same is true of the war between the Servians and Bulgarians. We have here heard no particulars of the conflict since leaving London —only some unreliable rumors—and there is no doubt that the full particulars reach London and New York daily. You will quite understand the matter when I tell you that the only item of news that has reached me, except the money and market reports, since leaving America, on the 7th inst., nearly one month, is that of the death of Horace B. Claflin. That item was cabled over the day I left London. If you want to feel isolated, and get out of the way of everything that touches humanity, come to Turkey.

How soon all this would change with the introduction of free schools, free speech, and a free press! But until some change comes in the government, which is liable to occur at any time, there is little hope of a better condition of things than now obtains.

Having spent but two days here, of course it has been quite impossible to obtain full and satisfactory information of the great city, and many places which it is desirable for a stranger to visit have been omitted.

LETTER III.

Leaving Constantinople—Observing Thanksgiving Day —The Excellent Defences of Constantinople—Arrival at Smyrna—One of the Oldest Cities of the World—A Description Thereof—The Bazaar and Its Peculiarities—The Turk's Creed—Display of Brigands' Heads—The Island of Chios—The Effect of Earthquakes—Samos, Patmos, and Rhodes—Then Direct for Cyprus—Beyrout—The American Presbyterian Mission there—Off for Baalbec by *Diligence*—An irrepressible Chicago Yankee—Ascending the Lebanon Mountains and on to Damascus—The Manufacture of Silk—The Ruins of Baalbec—Mt. Hermon in the Distance.

BEYROUT, SYRIA, December 13, 1885.

WE leave Constantinople, regretting that the arrangements for our journey preclude a longer visit at this most interesting old city. It is our first view of a distinctively Eastern civilization, and the sharp contrasts which everywhere meet the eye and ear, in comparison with the scenes so recently left behind at home, do not fail to produce a most decided impression upon the mind.

We embark on the Austrian Lloyds steamer *Hungaria*, leaving a small group at the American legation in the midst of Thanksgiving dinner; for Americans did not forget in this faraway land that it was Thanksgiving day at home, and on that occasion the little group who thus celebrated the day at Constantinople no doubt enjoyed themselves especially well, as their host was Hon. S. S. Cox, who is the very personification of wit, good humor, and patriotism.

As we leave the city we have an admirable view of the old wall and fortifications. We pass through the Sea of Marmora during the night, and early in the morning enter the Dardanelles, a long, narrow passage between the two continents. The distance across, at the narrowest point, is about one mile, and the passage is very strongly fortified.

One only need pass through the Bosphorus on the one side and the Dardanelles on the other to fully comprehend the admirable position of Constantinople for defence, and to cease to wonder why the Russians have not ere this accomplished their long-settled purpose of gaining possession of the city and the passage from the Black Sea to the Mediterranean; for these forts, aided by the Turkish navy, which is quite formidable, would be able to make a long resistance even without the aid of other navies,

which aid would be promptly rendered in such
an emergency. We now enter the archipelago
and begin at once to pass the numerous islands
which stud the coast, the names of many of
which are familiar to the readers of the New
Testament. Our steamer is very slow, making
only about nine or ten miles an hour; but the
cabin is homelike and sweet, the state-rooms
comfortable, and the table good. The cabin-
passengers are made up of Americans, English,
Austrians, French, Italians, Turks, Greeks, Armenians, etc. A venerable Turkish pasha, who
is travelling with his family, dines in the cabin,
while his wives—inferior beings—browse outside
on the deck, and seem to think it all right. The
deck-passengers contain most of the above mixture, together with many other possible and impossible varieties, great, lazy, black eunuchs, servants, peasants, men, women, children, and dogs
massed together in heterogeneous groups. Between the quarrelling and singing of the men
and women, the crying of the babies, and the
howling of the dogs, we have music (?) night
and day.

On the morning of the third day we arrive at
Smyrna, where we stop all day, delivering and
receiving goods. This is one of the oldest cities

in the world. It dates so far back that its origin is lost in mystery. The earliest record that exists of it is that it was destroyed by its enemies many centuries before Christ, and that it was rebuilt during the time of Alexander the Great, some three hundred and fifty years before the Christian era. During the last part of the first century a Christian church was established here, and about a century later Polycarp suffered martyrdom in this city. It is now the most important Asiatic seaport town on the Mediterranean. It looks much more enterprising and commercial than Constantinople.

The limited harbor, which is enclosed by a massive stone wall, built by French capital, is filled with steamers discharging and receiving freight. The exports are fruits, cotton, carpets, etc., and the imports are cotton goods, glass, hardware, steel, sugar, etc. All the passengers and goods are landed by barges, though there seems no good reason why they cannot be landed direct on the stone pier, except that they never have been.

Camels and men do the work of horses and carts. Many processions of camels are passing and repassing along the streets. Each line, of from six to twenty, connected by leading-strings, is conducted by a diminutive ass or by an Arab, and the animal seems to perform the duty quite as intelligently as the man.

The city is built compactly and in a substantial way. Its principal feature is the bazaar, which is the same old story over again—a series of little shops or stalls, filled with all sorts of Turkish goods, each presided over by a sharp Turk, the first article of whose business creed is to ask enough, and the second to get all he can. There are some interesting ruins on the brow of the hill just back of the city, which are said to be infested with brigands, so that it is unsafe to visit them without an escort.

A few months since an English gentleman residing here was captured by the brigands while on a hunting excursion, who held him, and demanded £15,000 for his ransom. His friends here raised some £1,500, and they gave him up for that sum. The Turkish government pursued them with a military force, captured and killed six of their number, and cut off their heads and placed three of them on the iron pickets of a fence in a public place in the city, and the other three inside the iron fence of the principal prison, in such a position that the people passing in the street could view them. I have purchased photos of the heads in these positions, for which the photographer demanded a high price, because he said he had to pay heavily to the Turkish officials for the exclusive privilege of copying them.

It seems that the brigands are greatly feared by the people, as no one will testify against them, even when they are caught, and it is morally certain that they are guilty. I was informed by the German Consul at Smyrna that the gentleman alluded to above, when summoned to appear in court subsequently to testify against some others of the band who were captured, was quite ready to swear that the heads belonged to some of his captors, but could not recognize the heads that were still on the shoulders of the other robbers, as he knew he would be murdered by the band if he did. This was not an exceptional case, for no one could be found who would testify against them.

Smyrna contains a population of some 200,000, of which more than one-half are Greeks, the balance being Turks, Jews, Armenians, English, French, etc.

Leaving Smyrna, we soon pass the island of Chios, where such devastation was wrought a few years ago by a terrible earthquake, in which over four thousand lives were lost, and which all will remember awakened great sympathy throughout the civilized world. The whole region is much disturbed from this cause. I am informed that several shocks occur at Smyrna every year. The island of Chios looks, as we pass it, like a series of barren mountains studded with cities and villages; but the valleys are said to be very fertile, producing abundantly wine, olives, oranges, and other fruits.

At this point the passage between the two continents is ten miles wide, and the scene from the deck of the steamer is magnificent. On the right are the towering mountains of Chios, and on the left the abrupt bluffs of the Asiatic coast, with a chain of high mountains in the background. About noon we pass the island of Samos, and later in the day the island of Patmos, a name very familiar to all readers of the Epistles of Paul. The town of Patmos is situated near the summit of a mountain on the island, and is crowned by an immense castle, apparently in ruins. Another day brings us to Rhodes, where we landed during the night, passing near the spot where stood the famed Colossus of Rhodes. We have now passed through the archipelago, an exceedingly interesting sail of three days, and are just entering the broad

Mediterranean Sea, in a direct course for the island of Cyprus.

At Larnica, the principal port of Cyprus, we are detained a whole day, thus making our trip from Constantinople to Beyrout, eleven hundred miles, occupy just a week, a sufficient time now to cross the Atlantic, nearly three times the distance. But I am already learning to curb my ambition and moderate my pace, a lesson which may be most useful to many a man accustomed to brave the rushing tide of business life, and struggle with ceaseless energy for its prizes.

The English now possess the island of Cyprus, paying to the Turkish government a certain stipulated sum annually.

Beyrout is a very old place. It is said to have been destroyed about two centuries before Christ, and to have been rebuilt by the Romans, who opened baths and theatres, and introduced gladiatorial combats. The manufacture of silk fabrics was established here during the third century. This is one of the oldest industries in this country, and still flourishes in many parts of Syria. Large numbers of the mulberry-tree are interspersed with fig and orange and olive trees.

Since 1860, the date of the great massacre at

Damascus, a large accession has been made to the population of Beyrout, very many of the Christian population having removed thither from the former place, and the city is said to now contain a population of about 80,000. The architecture and streets present a decidedly Oriental appearance, but there are some marks of Western civilization. There are many modern carriages passing in the streets, and the effect is odd and curious as they jostle the laden camel trains approaching and leaving the city.

The American Presbyterians established a mission here about fifty years ago, with branches in various parts of the East. Connected with this is a printing-office, a commercial school, a medical college, and a theological seminary, which affords superior advantages to foreign residents and others in educating their children. In an interview with the Rev. Dr. Jessup, one of the American missionaries, who has been stationed here over thirty years, I learn that they very seldom make any converts from Mohammedanism, which perhaps does not seem so very strange when we consider that the Mohammedan most firmly believes in and devoutly worships one God, and accepts Mohammed as his prophet, while the God the missionaries present to him requires explanation as to his composite nature and attributes, and the prophet of the Christian must be accepted as God, or at least only through him can God be approached.

Beyrout is the principal seaport of Syria, and is assuming considerable commercial importance, possessing one of the best bays for anchorage on the coast. The situation of the town, on a slight elevation and directly on the bay, is exceptionally fine, and the view gained from the deck of the steamer in approaching is indeed beautiful. The Lebanon range of mountains rises very abruptly from the edge of the town, stretching in both directions up and down the coast. It is terraced a considerable distance towards the summit and cultivated. There are many small villages in sight, the inhabitants all being engaged in cultivating grapes, oranges, figs, olives, and grain, which are all brought to Beyrout on mules for home consumption and for export.

We leave Beyrout for Baalbec at four A.M. by diligence, a curious conveyance, combining the features of an European railway-carriage, a Concord stage-coach, and an omnibus. It is drawn by six animals (three abreast), a mixture of species, but mostly of the mule persuasion. The nationality of the passengers is evidently as varied as is that of the animals which draw the vehicle—Americans, Europeans, and, for aught we know, "Cretes, Arabians, and dwellers in Mesopotamia," with a corresponding mixture of tongues.

The one saving clause for me is my Chicago friend, who is a study and a continual source of amusement. He is one of those versatile geniuses, which are peculiarly the product of America. Our minister at Constantinople, Hon. S. S. Cox, in introducing him to me, characterized him most happily as the "irrepressible Chicago Yankee." He has one of those peculiar, high-keyed voices, loud and self-assertive, which makes you laugh and get angry at the same time, and if you try to analyze the product you ascertain that you are more amused than angry, and so soon find yourself tempting him to further use of his powers. He has been travelling in Europe and Asia for more than a year, and speaks several languages, and so proves a godsend as a companion to one who speaks only English.

We ascend the main range of the Lebanon Mountains at once on leaving Beyrout. A distance of three or four miles brings us to a very high elevation, and the view of Beyrout and the

Mediterranean Sea from the summit is especially fine. From Beyrout to Damascus (about seventy miles) is a most substantial macadamized road, constructed by the French as a kind of memorial of the French expedition of 1860, and is the only similar road in Syria. Although the road is smooth and solid, it takes fourteen hours to make the seventy miles, so much of the distance is up-hill. All the traffic between Beyrout and Damascus passes over this road, much of the merchandise being transported by wagons. The camel and mule trains usually take the old track, which generally runs parallel, in order to avoid the tolls, which are very high. All kinds of enterprises and improvements that are inaugurated in this country are very expensive, mainly because the leading officials, who grant the privileges, have to be heavily bribed. But the expense falls on the people at last, for very heavy tolls have to be demanded. It is said that the French company owning the road divide fifteen per cent. annually on the capital invested.

The entire mountain sections seem barren and sterile, especially when viewed from a distance, but a nearer view discloses the fact that most of the surface of the mountain is terraced with stone walls and cultivated, the principal crop being grapes. The grape-vines are not trellised, as with us, but lie flat on the ground, looking at a little distance like great black serpents. Grapes here are abundant and cheap, and they are exceedingly fine, being entirely ripe and of most delicious flavor, contrasting favorably with the table grapes in our own country, which are seldom dead ripe, and almost always have a crude acid in the centre. These grapes are found in abundance on every table, and constitute one course at dinner, together with oranges and figs, which are also very delicious.

We pass many groves of the mulberry-tree, for one of the principal industries of this part of Syria is the manufacture of silk. But it seems remarkable to an American that it should all be made by hand in exactly the same way it has been made for hundreds of years. No steam-power, no improved machinery. As an example, showing the different results attained by the improved machinery of England and the United States, and the crude methods still prevailing here, I was told that it takes a man an entire day to weave a small pocket-handkerchief that retails for fifty cents.

At Shtora, some thirty miles from Beyrout, we diverge from the main road and go twenty-five miles to the left to visit Baalbec. The road is much inferior to the French road, but we compass the distance by carriage in five hours. We pass through a fertile valley, some eighty or ninety miles long and fifteen to twenty miles wide, through the centre of which runs the Litany River, which rises in the mountains and passes through the ruins at Baalbec. It is a small stream, and is used through the entire valley for purposes of irrigation. We first see the ruins at Baalbec some fifteen miles before we reach the spot. In passing through this valley we have a fine view of Mount Hermon in the far distance, the highest mountain in Syria, with its summit covered with snow. But here is Baalbec.

LETTER IV.

The Earliest Records of Baalbec—Something about its Ruins—The Great Temple of the Sun, with a Description of its Ruins—Most of the Holy Places Mythical—A Mingling of Ancient and Modern Work—A Smaller Temple also Dedicated to the Sun—The Journey to Damascus Resumed.

BAALBEC, SYRIA, Dec. 15, 1885.

THE earliest written records we have of Baalbec occur in the third century of the Christian era, and there is little doubt it was built by the Romans, although there are various mythical claims put forth as to its origin, some of which carry it back to a very much earlier period. One account is to the effect that it was built by Uz, who was the grandson of Shem. The Arabs claim that the great temple was built by Solomon, and that it was afterwards converted into a citadel, and there are records extant showing that it was used as a fortress during the middle ages. The temple was called Heliopolis by the Greeks, who supposed that it was built by the worshippers of the sun. History records that the Christians were here persecuted from time to time during the third and fourth centuries, and it is claimed that it was destroyed by

Constantine. There is little doubt that it was destroyed about that period, and by the Christians.

In viewing these stately ruins now, and trying to form some faint conception of the grandeur of the original structures, and remembering that the work of destruction was performed by the Christians, one can naturally be a little more tolerant with the Mohammedans who defaced the Christian churches at Constantinople when they gained the possession of them by destroying the representations of Christ and the saints and angels, and all the mottoes and emblems of Christianity. They at least left the structures intact, which stand to-day the wonder and admiration of the world. The ruins of Baalbec were discovered during the sixteenth century by Europeans. Since that period the work of destruction has been completed by earthquakes, which have occurred at various periods. In view of such a history, covering so many centuries, during which these colossal buildings were reared and their destruction consummated, both by human agencies and the decay of passing cycles, one must be dull indeed who can stand in such a presence unmoved.

I had heard and read much of the ruins of

Baalbec, and there is nothing embraced in my visit to this historic land which I had anticipated with so much interest. I have seen nothing thus far, nor do I expect to, affording such satisfaction as this visit to Baalbec. Most of the holy places, except the sites of cities and mountains, and probably all of the numerous relics, are mythical and spurious. But here is a "real presence," requiring no stretching of your faith or taxing of your credulity. You can read much of the history of the place in the records lying before you. Your feet press them, your eyes behold them. Neither the passions of men inspired by the fiercest fanatical zeal nor the decay of centuries has been able to efface the record. Let me now attempt a brief description, which may give some faint conception of these stupendous ruins.

In visiting this place the first thought that occurs to one is the wonder how such a city should have been in such a location, on the edge of an open plain far off in the interior. But everything connected with its history is so enshrouded in mystery, all positive record of its origin having been destroyed, that we can only conjecture. That it dates far back of the Christian era there can be no doubt.

The principal group of the ruins is that formed by the remains of the great Temple of the Sun. The grand entrance faces the south. The portico was thirty-six feet wide and had twelve columns in front, the bases of which only are preserved. On each side, and connected with the portico by doors, are large, square chambers, built of solid stone, and richly ornamented with the most elaborate carving. These side structures were at one period converted into fortified towers.

From this grand entrance we pass into a large hexagonal court two hundred feet long and two hundred and fifty feet wide. Still within this, and approached by massive gateways, lies the great inner court, which is nearly four hundred feet wide by four hundred and fifty feet long. This court is surrounded by an exceedingly massive wall containing many highly ornamental chambers. All this is only the approach to the great temple, which we reach by passages on the north side of the great court just described.

Very little remains in its original position of this wonderful structure, but some description of the portion still standing and of the remains scattered about will help to form an idea of its vast proportions and wonderful beauty. Six columns on one side only remain in position. We caught a view of these many miles before reaching the city. They are sixty feet in height and seven and a half feet in diameter, standing on bases seven feet high, and crowned with a cornice, seventeen feet high, carved in the most elaborate and artistic manner. The three blocks composing each column are held together by an immense iron bar passing through their centre. The Arabs and Turks have mutilated the columns in several places in their efforts to remove the bars of iron. There were originally nineteen of these columns on each side and ten on each end of the temple. The six now standing look very insecure, and seem liable to fall at any time. The ruins of these columns lie scattered about in great confusion.

So complete is the destruction of the great temple which these massive columns surrounded that its form and special features can only be conjectured. The foundations of it stood about fifty feet above the surrounding plain upon which the city was built. Outside of all, and twenty-nine feet distant from the temple, stands an outer wall. This is called the "Cyclopean wall," from the size of some of the blocks of which it is built. These stones now demand our special attention. Everybody has heard of these wonderful blocks of stone, but only seeing them can convey an adequate conception of their size. There are three of them in this wall, each thirteen feet high, and about the same in width, and some sixty-four feet long, and, being placed end to end in the wall, they occupy the space of about two hundred feet of its length, which is but a moderate fraction of the entire length of the wall on the north side of the main temple. This portion of the outer wall was evidently unfinished, as these big stones, which were placed in the wall nineteen feet above the ground, undoubtedly formed the top layer of the original structure, although the Turks had (most likely some centuries after the temple was built) piled many courses of huge blocks (evidently fragments of the original temple) above these three great blocks in the wall. That this part of the wall is modern, and built by unskilled hands, is perfectly evident, as the eye detects here the base of a column and there a cornice, finished with the exquisite skill of the original builders, mingled with plain blocks of stone and without any apparent design.

Another indication that this wall was unfinished is that there is a huge block lying at the quarry, about a mile from the building, made evidently to match those already set in the wall. This stone is seventy-one feet long, thirteen feet wide, fourteen feet high. There is no mistaking its proportions, as it lies above the ground, and can be easily measured. Some idea may be formed of the size of this block by conceiving of a room thirteen feet wide, fourteen feet high, and seventy-one feet long, and then realizing that this stone will exactly fill the space. The great marvel is how these immense blocks were removed from the quarry, transported nearly a mile, and hoisted nineteen feet from the ground into the wall. And there seems now little chance of our ever ascertaining. It appears impossible to accomplish this feat today, with all the modern appliances of steam machinery, including hydraulic power, of which we can hardly suppose the ancients possessed any knowledge.

On the west side and very near the great temple stands a much smaller one, also dedicated to the Sun. This building is in a better state of preservation, and is also surrounded by a row of magnificent columns, fifteen on each side, and eight on each end. Some of these are still standing, many are lying scattered on the ground, and one has lodged, in falling, against the main wall of the building. It has doubtless stood in that position for centuries, with one end resting upon the floor and the other end leaning against the wall. I will not attempt a minute description of this smaller temple. It was evidently built with the same skilful hands, and perhaps for the same general purpose.

Our hotel here, which is a solid stone structure from bottom to top, was made from the scattered fragments of the great temple. Immense quantities of the materials composing the original structures have been removed and thus utilized.

We return by the same route to Shtora and resume our journey to Damascus, some account of which will comprise our next letter.

LETTER V.

Back to Shtora—By Diligence to Damascus—Its Famed Gardens—A Cool Reception, but a Fire and Good Dinner Warm us—The Oldest City in Palestine—Its Celebrated Blades and Silk Manufactures—All Labor-Saving Machinery Resisted—The Mosques—Head of John the Baptist—The Great Bazaar—The "East Gate of the City"—House of Ananias—Paul's Prison—The Private Houses—Witnessing the Rite of Circumcision—The House of Naaman—Massacre of 1860—It was Encouraged by the Turkish Government—An Interesting Episode.

DAMASCUS, SYRIA, Dec. 20, 1885.

LEAVING Baalbec at five o'clock A.M. we retrace our steps to Shtora, reaching that place in time to get our lunch and take the diligence for Damascus. First we cross the valley between the two ranges of mountains, and then ascend and cross the Anti-Lebanon range. All the distance we have the same splendid macadamized road. We have as fellow-passengers the Turkish pasha, who, with his harem, came in the steamer with us to Beyrout. At the last station before reaching Damascus he transferred his retinue to a carriage, which was in waiting, and made the entry into the city in grand style, while the rest of us stuck to the democratic diligence.

We are now in the suburbs, and have a fine view of the famed gardens of Damascus, though for the most part they are enclosed by high, massive stone walls, and we can only get a view of them from elevated points of the road. The gardens have been celebrated for thousands of years. They owe their wonderful luxuriance mainly to the river that runs through the middle of the city, which is diverted, at various suitable points, into six canals, three on each side of the stream, which furnish every house and grounds in the city with an abundance of pure, fresh water. After passing through so much barren-looking mountain scenery, it is very refreshing to come suddenly upon a spot so delightfully green and luxuriant—like an oasis in the desert.

Damascus being situated among the mountains and at a considerable elevation above the Mediterranean, it is much colder than at Beyrout. On our arrival at the hotel, being chilled by the cold air, we inquired for a fire. The landlord answered: "We have no fire; we never light our fires till after the Christmas holidays." But after we had rather forcibly suggested that a hotel was intended for the comfort and convenience of travellers, and that just now we were very uncomfortable, he rather reluctantly ordered a fire to be kindled in a very diminutive stove in the large and high dining-room. So we carried our point, succeeding in making an innovation in a country where innovations are unpopular, and, between the fire and a good dinner, got warm. Notwithstanding this rather cool reception on our arrival, we found the Victoria Hotel much the best house we have encountered since leaving Europe.

Damascus is said to be the oldest city in Palestine. Mention is made of it in the book of Genesis, but no hint is given as to its origin. It acquired great importance at a very early age from being the starting-point of the caravan trade with Persia and various parts of the East. The manufacture of the famed Damascus blades was established here at a very early date, also the manufacture of silk fabrics. The former trade was lost to the city in the year 1300, when it was plundered by the Tartars and the famous armorers were captured and carried to Samarcand, where the blades are still made; and the latter has been much encroached upon since the massacre of the Christians in 1860, as both the manufacture and sale of silk goods was largely in the hands of the Christians, and many of those who escaped with their lives would not resume their business and residence here, but moved to Beyrout and other places.

Here, as everywhere in this country, the introduction of labor-saving machinery is steadily resisted. Exactly the same primitive methods prevail that have been used for four thousand years. An operative can weave only one small silk handkerchief in a day; but it would be quite impossible to introduce a power loom with which he could weave thirty or forty in the same length of time.

The two leading physical features of the city are the mosques and the great bazaar. There are said to be three hundred of the former scattered in all parts of the city. The great mosque is said to have been erected upon the site of a heathen temple. It was built early in the Christian era, and was formerly known as "the Church of St. John," as it contained a casket with the head of John the Baptist. A relic is now shown which the people here swear is the veritable head that was presented to Herodius on a charger. We have no doubt it will be quite safe to receive this claim with many degrees of allowance.

The bazaar occupies an immense area, embracing the "street called Straight," which is a straight, wide avenue, covered with a roof, and said to be a mile long. In this bazaar nearly all the goods that are offered for sale are made. It is well worth an exhaustive visit, but a detailed description would hardly be interesting.

One of the most striking old land-marks is the "east gate of the city." The centre gateway is thirty-eight feet high and twenty feet wide, with a smaller gate each side. Not far from this gate is situated the house of Ananias, at least so tradition has it. Its evident age would seem to entitle it to that distinction. There is a small private chapel under the court-yard, used by the Roman Catholics, who have possession of the premises. One wonders that Ananias and Saphira had not said their prayers to better effect, and so been fortified against the sin of lying. May it not be that this was the incipiency of the modern Christian fashion of committing the same sin? If the same penalty were attached to the sin in this Christian age, would there not be an alarming decrease in the population? We saw the prison where Paul was said to have been confined, and the place where the window was located by which he was let down by the wall in a basket and so made his escape. Near by was the tomb of the keeper of the prison, who was put to death by order of the king because he allowed his prisoner to escape.

We visited several other points of interest, the Greek church, the Arch of Triumph, and the big plane-tree, called the "Hangman's Tree," which is forty-eight feet in circumference at the largest part of the trunk, etc., etc. We also gained admission into two private houses of wealthy citizens—one a rich Jewish banker and the other a Christian gentleman. They were both spacious and magnificent in the interiors but very commonplace outside. While we were examining the house of the Jew a procession of common-looking people came into the inner court from the street bearing flowers and bringing a boy-baby eight days old. They had brought the child to be circumcised, as the rich man allowed his poor brethren to use his house for that purpose. The priest was waiting in a room up-stairs, to which the procession proceeded. Our dragoman said we could go in, so we pressed in among the rest and witnessed the performance of the rite of circumcision.

We passed the house of Naaman, as it is called, a hospital for lepers, supposed to be on the site of Naaman's house. It has at present some twelve or fifteen unfortunates afflicted with that dreadful malady, and is supported by charity. Near by is the large tomb where all the remains of the victims of the terrible massacre of 1860 were deposited.

As many, especially so far away as America, have, after a lapse of a quarter of a century, a rather indefinite idea of the tragedy enacted here in 1860, I will give a brief account of the massacre, with some allusions to the events which led to it and culminated in that awful butchery. The causes did not originate in Damascus, but in a large mountain district called "The Lebanon," which lies near the sea-coast, and between Damascus and Beyrout. This section was inhabited by Druses and Maronites, one-third of the population belonging to the former sect and two thirds to the latter. The Druses have existed as a sect since the eleventh century, and take their name from a leader of that period named Darazi. His system was full of mysteries, and threw a cloak over the indulgences of the worst passions of human nature. They are governed by a temporal and spiritual chief or sheik, each having absolute power in his realm. They observe great secrecy in their worship, and are ever on the defensive when approached on the subject of their belief and religious rites. Their acts show plainly enough that their belief is a terrible embodiment of savagery and lust.

By their enemies it is said that the religion of the Druses allows certain gross immoralities and cruel practices, but they keep everything so secret that little can be known except what may be inferred from their outward lives and manners. They have a peculiar method of divorce. The husband has the power to divorce his wife at any time. He simply bids her go back to her family, using a certain form of words, and henceforth she must not speak to him or look at him. The husband, however, is not entirely absolved from supporting her, for in the last extremity he must see that she is supplied. But practically, it is said, the husband seldom does anything in that way.

While stopping in a Druse village as the guest of a gentleman who has a residence there, we learned that the cook was a divorced wife of the spiritual sheik of the village, and, as she saw him coming to the house, she instantly abandoned her work and hid herself, and remained hidden during the visit. The Turkish government, to which the sect owes allegiance and pays taxes, recognizes these divorces. At one period the Druses were so strongly established in southern Lebanon that the entire range was called the mountain of the Druses. The northern portion was occupied by the Christian sect of the Maronites. They were named after their master, one Maron. They were long estranged from the Roman Catholic Church, but finally gave their adhesion to it.

The pope overlooked many irregularities in them, and contented himself with their acknowledgment of their allegiance to him. Over a century ago a bitter feud originated between these sects, in consequence of the conversion of two important personages to the Maronite faith. This feud has never been healed, and paved the way to the terrible massacres of 1840 and 1860. It is beyond all question that the Turkish government have always directly encouraged the dissensions between those two sects, and have ever been ready to help the Druses in their efforts to exterminate the Maronites (Christians). Indeed, it is positively proven that on several occasions, when the Druses and the Maronites were in collision, they secretly furnished arms to both parties. The animus with which pride of race and the Mohammedan religion inspires the Turk is indescribable, and accounts in some degree for their treachery and cruelty in striving to circumvent and undermine any form of Christianity seeking to gain foothold among them.

This brief preliminary explanation furnishes the key to the terrible slaughter of the Maronites at Damascus in 1860, which so shocked the civilized world everywhere. The origin of this massacre was the bitter feud between the Druses and the Maronites of the Lebanon, and the outbreak at Damascus did not occur until more than a month of slaughter and pillage had been accomplished in the Lebanon, and it has been abundantly proved that the Mohammedans in Damascus were encouraged by the Turkish government in this dreadful work, and there is very little doubt that a direct order was given to that end.

The six great Christian powers of Europe now interfered and selected the governor-general of the Lebanon. The Porte had to submit. One of the provisions of this arrangement is, that the taxes for the whole province shall be paid in one sum, instead of being collected, as previously, directly by the Turkish government. This arrangement works admirably, and since its adoption peace and great prosperity prevail.

When the revulsion came after the interference of the Christian powers, large demands were made by those Christians who survived the massacre at Damascus, and, as they were backed by the attitude of the powers, large sums were paid by the rich Mohammedan merchants; and it is said that many of them were entirely ruined, while some of the Christians, who had not really suffered seriously, were enriched from that source. Many Christians, who had grudges against Turks or owed them money, took advantage of the change in the course of events, and sated their revenge or got absolved from their obligations. The Christian quarter of the city, which was devastated and burned, has been mostly rebuilt during the twenty-five years that have since transpired.

A most interesting episode of the great massacre occurred towards its close. A very prominent Bedouin sheik, who exercised great control over this part of Syria, took a bold stand at the moment when the Christians of Haifa, Acre, Nazareth, and other towns were daily expecting the deadly attack, and sent a faithful follower to each place and force enough to awe the Moslem populace, as well as the authorities, and by this decisive measure stopped the movement against the Christians and saved their lives. But I am sorry to add that the moment the siege was over the Christians (?) returned to their avocations, never even thanking their deliverer. And this man was a wild Bedouin, who could neither read nor write. He afterwards became very poor, and died only two weeks ago in great poverty.

LETTER VI.

Jaffa, the Joppa of Scripture—The House of Simon, the Tanner—Off for Jerusalem—Something about Ramleh—The Church of the Nativity at Bethlehem, and the Christmas Celebration thereat: the Legends connected therewith—The Plain of Bethlehem—The Field of Boaz—Jerusalem, City of the Great King—What was Seen on a Tour through it—A Few Words about the American Consul.

JERUSALEM, December 25, 1885.

JAFFA, called in Scripture Joppa, one of the principal ports of Palestine, is situated on a high bluff, and presents a picturesque appearance as the traveller approaches it by steamer. It has no harbor, and when it is very rough the steamers cannot land passengers, and they are often carried by to their great inconvenience. As in all the ports of Palestine, passengers and goods are landed by small boats, while the vessel lies in the open sea, some quarter of a mile from the shore. The city is small and dirty. The streets are narrow and very crooked. One of the principal thoroughfares we found, on measurement, to be only six feet wide from house to house, with no sidewalks, of course. About the only claim the city has to distinction on the score of antiquities is the possession of the house of "Simon, the tanner," which we have visited. It is a strongly-built old house, and looks as though it might be either five hundred or five thousand years old.

We leave Jaffa for Jerusalem early on the morning of December 24, in a pouring rain, being desirous of visiting Bethlehem and witnessing the ceremonies in the Church of the Nativity on Christmas day. We pass several interesting spots on the road. At Ramleh is a high, old tower, which is said to be all that remains of an ancient Turkish mosque, and that it was erected by the Crusaders. There is a tradition that forty Christian martyrs, who were precipitated from its summit, now repose beneath in a tomb excavated for that purpose. Further along our dragoman points out the field where Samson tied the firebrands to the foxes' tails, and sent them, all ablaze, into the fields of ripened corn belonging to the Philistines; also the vale of Ajalon, where Joshua commanded the sun and moon to stand still while the Israelites slew the hosts of the enemy.

On the morning of the 25th we leave Jerusalem in a drenching rain and arrive in one hour at Bethlehem, in season to witness the celebration of the great Mass which the Roman Catholics hold on Christmas morning in their chapel in the Church of the Nativity. The music is fine and the ceremonials elaborate and, to us, incomprehensible.

The Church of the Nativity is supposed to occupy the very spot where Christ was born, and is in the joint possession of the Roman Catholics, the Greeks, and the Armenians, each having a chapel in the church edifice. On Christmas day these three sects occupy by turns the small chapel and altar in the basement, containing the manger in which Christ was born, so that it is in use during the whole twenty-four hours. The Greek priests were just moving out of the chapel as we entered. The Roman Catholic clergy entered immediately, and took possession with all their machinery of worship, burning of incense, etc. After these came the Armenians with their mumble-jumble. From all that is said of the rivalries and bickerings of these three sects, it is to be feared that they are not very thoroughly permeated with the spirit of Him whose birth they thus celebrate.

The manger is deep down under the church, and is claimed to be the identical one in which Christ was born. Near the manger is the spot where the wise men stood when they came from the East to worship Him, and the exact point over which the star stood is represented by a metal star on the floor. Near by, and approached by a dark passage, is the milk-cave, where the Virgin spent one night previous to the flight into Egypt, and the legend is that one drop of milk exuded from her breast here, and the entire surface of the stone composing the cave immediately turned white, and that any woman who does not have a supply for her babe will at once find the fountain opened by rubbing a fragment of this stone upon her breast. I could not, however, help observing that the whole formation was limestone, and that the color of the stone walls in the cave was identical with that of all the surrounding stones.

From the brow of the hill on the edge of the city we look down upon the plains of Bethlehem, where the "shepherds watched their flocks by night," also upon the field of Boaz, where Ruth gleaned after the reapers.

Bethlehem is a compact little city of about 5,000 inhabitants, presenting the general appearance of the cities of Palestine: solid stone houses with stone or tiled roofs; narrow, crooked, and very dirty streets. The sewerage is above ground, and no pains seem to be taken to convey away the accumulated filth. Returning to Jerusalem we pass the tomb of Rachel, situated immediately upon the road between the two cities.

Jerusalem! City of the great King, city of the Christian's affection, city of the Jew's passionate idolatry, scene of the public ministry of Christ and of His death! This is indeed hallowed ground. It is no wonder that so many pilgrims wend their way thither with pious zeal, or that so many aged Jews return here to die. The city now contains 40,000 inhabitants, and more than half are Jews, the proportion of their race having greatly increased during the last few years. Many very poor Jews return here, large numbers being sent by wealthy Jews of England and by different societies which have interested themselves in their behalf.

It has occurred to me that next to an actual visit to these scenes would be the plain description of an eye-witness, and some rehearsal of the claims made for them by their custodians. By this means the reader can form some idea as to which are genuine or which are spurious.

Our first view of the city, gained from the roof of our hotel, of course within the walls, is sadly disappointing. It is really a scene of desolation. Except a few domes and prominent buildings, it seems to be really a city of ruins, though the area within the walls is small, and they have had many centuries in which to rebuild. When one thinks of a city of which it could be said—

> "Glorious things of thee are spoken,
> Zion! city of our God"—

and then views the modern city, with its narrow, crooked, and dirty streets; with its heaps of rubbish and total absence of all sanitary appliances; with its teeming population, whose faces, for the most part, look pale and pinched and wan, as if some fell disease had already secured them as victims, the contrast between the pictures of the old and the realities of the modern city is, indeed, most striking. Hence a cursory view of the city, or a superficial examination of its contents, discloses little towards realizing one's preconceived idea of its glories and its beauties.

The Jerusalem of two thousand years ago can only be in any degree realized by patient research far beneath the surface which modern civilization has, during the lapse of many centuries, accreted above the glorious ancient city. All the sacred spots within the walls are covered with strata after strata of rubbish, and above all with a shroud of rottenness woven by the seething population now covering its surface. Hence, in the tour we now propose through the city and its surroundings, we shall instinctively take, with "many grains of allowance," most of the statements that will be glibly told us of the sacred spots and of the incidents that have occurred upon them, and we may expect to be pained by the exhibition of the wild superstition, the fanaticism, and the insane jealousies of the numerous religious sects which make up modern Jerusalem.

We make our home while in the city at the Mediterranean Hotel, which is the leading one of the city, and really one of the best houses we have found in this country. One must not expect to find what we in America or England call "first-class" accommodations. We meet here many Americans and English, and get acquainted with each other with wonderful facility. Indeed, the circle seems to comprise a harmonious and jolly family group.

At dinner we are presided over by the American consul, Mr. Merrill, who makes the hotel his home. He and his accomplished wife are the life of the circle, and they are exceedingly attentive to all strangers, and of course look especially after the welfare of Americans.

It is much to be regretted that the President has appointed an Arab as Mr. Merrill's successor, and especially as he seems to be a man without character or reliability. He has just arrived from America. But it seems that he has not been confirmed by the Senate, and everybody here is hoping that he will not be. But even if he should be confirmed, it is stated that the sultan will not recognize him as American minister, because he becomes a Turkish subject the moment he touches the soil here, as he has only been absent in America some six or seven years. So it is almost sure that Mr. Merrill will remain at his post for some time, and all here who know him best, and are fully acquainted with the facts, sincerely hope that no one may be sent to replace him. He is in every way admirably adapted to fill the position, and has been here just long enough to become acquainted with its duties, and, moreover, he takes a great interest in the country and its resources, and is making strenuous efforts for its development by endeavoring to inaugurate an exchange of products between Palestine and America. Besides, he is quite a scientist, and is making a fine ornithological collection, which is already extensive, and contains many rare specimens. It seems a great pity that our capable and level-headed President should disturb such a man in such a position, and, from his well-known views on the question of civil service, there can be little doubt that this removal has been made without fully realizing the facts of the case.

LETTER VII.

Further Descriptions in and about Jerusalem—Solomon's Temple
—Mosque of Omar—The Holy Rock where Abraham Offered
up Isaac—Mosque of El Aksa—Christ's Cradle—Church of
the Sepulchre—Warring Sects—The Hill of Calvary—Other
Sacred Spots and Relics—Remarkable Ruins—Church of St.
Ann—Pool of Bethesda—Tombs of the Kings—The Brook
Kedron—Mount of Olives—Pool of Siloam and other Sacred
Places—The German Colony—Back to Jaffa.

JERUSALEM, Dec. 30, 1885.

THE limits allowed in which to record the impressions of a traveller visiting these sacred places necessarily preclude anything like a historical sketch of them. The subject has been exhaustively treated by many different writers, who have made long and critical examinations of the different localities, aided by the extensive excavations that have been made deep down below the surface of the modern city. The oblong space known as the Haram claims the special attention of the visitor from the undoubted fact that it contains somewhere within its limits the site of the original temple built by Solomon. The Haram occupies something like one-sixth of the area of the entire city within the walls, and is situated in the southeast corner thereof.

Having fulfilled the necessary conditions to secure our entrance to the enclosure, we proceed thither with our dragoman, a soldier furnished by the Turkish authorities, and the cawass of the American Consul. We first visit the Mosque of Omar, which is the chief point of attraction, and stands nearly in the centre of the space comprising the Haram. This was the spot selected by Solomon for the erection of the great temple, and by David for the erection of an altar, and is claimed to have been the place of sacrifice as far back as the time of Abraham.

The principal point of interest is the immense natural rock which is situated directly under the dome of the mosque. This is called the Holy Rock. It is about sixty feet long by forty feet wide, and stands some six feet higher than the marble pavement of the mosque. From time immemorial it has been regarded as a sacred rock. The Jews have a tradition that it was the altar upon which Abraham was about to sacrifice Isaac. They also believe that the ark of the covenant once rested here, and that it now lies buried somewhere near. The Mohammedans believe that this rock hangs over an abyss without any support, and that it is the centre of the world.

There is a large excavation under the centre of the rock, a room occupying an area equal to more than half the size of the rock itself, which we enter by steps leading down into it. It has evidently been excavated from the solid rock, as the great rock itself forms its roof, and the floor is also rock. The sides are enclosed by an artificial wall, evidently not of stone. The attendant tapped on this partition to show us that it was hollow beyond, and to corroborate the claim that the great rock hangs in mid-air with no support. But he was careful not to give us a glimpse behind this partition to enable us to see whether the rock had any visible support. His faith was evidently strong enough to convince *him* that it had not ; but we unbelievers strongly suspected that the great rock would be found to have some connection with the adjoining mass of rock. There is a large hole through which Mohammed ascended into heaven on his favorite horse after he had prayed here. The Mohammedans tell many other wonderful stories about this great rock. On the four sides of the cave, under the rock, the guide shows us four altars, said to belong to David, Solomon, Abraham, and Elijah.

The Mosque of Omar is a very old building, and the architecture is most satisfying and harmonious. The windows and the mosaics are exceedingly rich. The latter are composed of small cubes of colored glass, and this work dates from the tenth and eleventh centuries. The windows bear the name of Soliman, and date 1528. We are shown, under a small tower, the footprint of Mohammed, also some hairs from his beard.

Within the Haram enclosure is the Mosque of El Aksa, also a very old and remarkable pile. The basement is specially interesting, and contains wonderful massive masonry and pillars. Near by we descend a long flight of steps and enter a small Mohammedan chapel, where we are shown the cradle of Christ, cut out of stone. This place was also, according to the legend, the dwelling of the aged Simeon. The Virgin is said to have spent a short time here after the presentation in the temple. At another angle of the grounds, and deep down under the surface, are the stables of Solomon, consisting of spacious vaults, twenty-eight feet high, and resting upon one hundred stone pillars.

We visit the Church of the Sepulchre, around which cluster so many interesting associations, a point of extraordinary attraction to all tourists. There are various, probably mythical, stories told of the buildings that have been erected here and destroyed between the time of Chri t and the present period, and it is stated that the foundations of the present structure were laid by the Crusaders. Among these stories, historians assert that Helena, the mother of Constantine, being divinely inspired, discovered not only the holy sepulchre but the cross of Christ on this spot; and we are shown the very room where the cross was found, and a seat at the side where Helena sat and directed the workmen who were making the excavations.

The present structure is only in part the work of the Crusaders. Having been seriously injured by a fire in 1808, the dome fell in and crushed the sepulchre. The Greeks and Armenians together rebuilt the church and restored the sepulchre. These two sects, together with the Roman Catholics, now control the building and the sepulchre. These three sects all raise their banners over the holy sepulchre, and are always ready to fight for the control. Indeed, on feast days, and especially at Easter, the Turkish government surround the sepulchre with a double cordon of soldiers, to prevent the Christians from murdering each other in their frantic efforts to secure precedence.

This dissension among the Christian sects, of which there are nine in Jerusalem altogether, is scandalous, and is especially noticed by all travellers. They cannot agree, even in so small a matter as the time of their church clocks. Each party asks the others to adopt their time, and all stoutly refuse. So there are so many kinds of time in the city that great confusion is the consequence. One is very apt, in view of these and kindred facts, to wonder how long it will take to convert the world to Christianity.

Only a few feet from the tomb, and in the same large room, is the hill of Calvary. This is a kind of gallery, fourteen and a half feet higher than the floor of the church; and although the church has been, at least once, devastated by fire, and although this gallery or platform, now called Mount Calvary, has been built upon the spot, and evidently must be many feet from the original ground, as it is well known that the city which stood here at that date was far below the Jerusalem of to-day, yet they show the very hole in the rock in which the cross of Christ was inserted, as well as of those of the crosses on which the two thieves were crucified, each about five feet distance.

There seems to have been an effort to cluster under the roof of this church as many of the sacred spots and relics as possible, and in many respects the effort appears to have been strained. A few of these places and objects are mentioned below to convey some idea of the claims made in this regard: "The place of division," where the soldiers cast lots for His garments; the tomb of Joseph of Arimathea; the tomb of Nicodemus; the Chapel of the Apparition; fragments of the pillar where Christ sat when they put the crown of thorns on His head; the grated window where Mary stood and looked upon Christ on the cross; the "rent" in the rock; the tomb of Adam; the spot where the earth was taken of which Adam was made; the sword and spears of the chief of the Crusaders. These, and many other similar things, are shown and explained in detail.

Leaving the church, we now visit several other interesting localities within the city walls. The Via Dolorosa represents the path travelled by Christ bearing His cross, along which are pointed out the different stations: the place where His mother looked upon her Son as He passed, bearing the cross, the places where He fell under the weight of the cross, the print of His hand on the stone wall against which He pressed it as He fell, etc.

We next visit some remarkable ruins, called the "Hospital of the Knights of Saint John," which have been unveiled by recent excavations. At one point we could see below the surface two stories of arches, each at least twenty feet high, and near by two similar arches above ground, all having been disclosed by digging from the surface. This gives a vivid glimpse of what ancient Jerusalem was, and a hint where to look for it.

Near by is the Church of St. Ann, the mother of the Virgin Mary. Here the very spot where the Virgin was born is marked by a small chapel. Opposite the latter and against the city wall is the Pool of Bethesda, now simply a vast depression some fifty feet deep, with no water, and at present used as a receptacle of the filth and débris of the city streets, and so being gradually filled up. We were also shown "the house of Caiphas, the high-priest," where Christ was brought and imprisoned, and the stone which the angel rolled away from the mouth of the tomb. The city is full of similar places, each having its clearly defined legend, which the people appear to implicitly accept, partly, perhaps, from its having become an "oft-told tale."

Passing out of the Jaffa gate, we now make an entire circuit of the city, visiting several places worthy of mention, in the following order: "The tombs of the kings," which are wonderful specimens of patient working, being excavated from solid rock far down below the surface. They have long since been rifled of their contents. The hill of Calvary, supposed to be the real Golgotha. Jeremiah's cave, now a Mohammedan burying-ground. Quarries under the city, very extensive and interesting, said to contain a mile of subterranean chambers. The brook Kedron (in the valley of Jehoshaphat), now entirely dry; no longer "the sweet, gliding Kedron."

Crossing the Kedron, we come to the tomb of the Virgin, which is held in great reverence. It is reached by passing down a long flight of wide stone steps. In the same enclosure we are shown the tomb of the mother of the Virgin and the tomb of Joseph.

We next come to the place where Stephen was stoned. The Garden of Gethsemane is a spot of exceeding interest, a small, square enclosure of about half an acre, surrounded by a wall, and nicely cared for by the Latin monks who are in charge. It contains several large and very old olive-trees, said to have stood there since the time of Christ, also beds of flowers which are cultivated by the monks. The place where the Lord "found His disciples sleeping" is near by.

We now ascend the Mount of Olives, a very high hill, commanding a fine view of Jerusalem, as well as of the Dead Sea in the distance. There is no question about the authenticity of this spot, and so one feels that he is indeed treading on sacred ground. An adjoining height is pointed out as the camping-ground of Titus when he besieged Jerusalem.

Descending the hill we come to the tombs of Absalom and Jehoshaphat, and passing the Pool of Siloam we enter the city again by the Jaffa gate. We have spent a week in Jerusalem, and have visited most of the sacred places, but of course we have made in that brief space only a cursory examination of them.

Before leaving the city we make a visit to

the German colony, which is located about one mile from the city proper, in the direction of Bethlehem. This is a branch of the colony settled at Haifa, of which I propose to speak in a future letter. They are a very worthy and reliable people, industrious and thriving. Everything about their settlement is in striking contrast with all that surrounds them. They have commenced the manufacture of wines on a somewhat extensive scale, have built large vaults, and are already exporting it to Europe and America in considerable quantities. A New York house keeps several brands of these wines, and finds a ready sale for them.

Leaving the city and returning to the sea-coast by the same route that we came, we take a "last, lingering look" before we descend the mountains that intervene, and in nine hours we are once more at Jaffa.

LETTER VIII.

From Haifa to Nazareth—First View of the City—At the Latin Convent and Monastery—The House and Kitchen of the Virgin—Church of the Annunciation—A Lesson for Christians of Europe and America—Old Greek Church—The Well of Mary—Orphan Asylum for Girls—Back to the Dirty City—Among the Native Artisans—An Arab Wedding—Cana of Galilee—The New Church there.

HAIFA, January 10, 1886.

IN conformity with our purpose of visiting Nazareth we make up a little party at this place, which is situated on the bay of Acre, and leave early in the morning by a very fair wagon-road, which was made about ten years since by the German colonists of Haifa. About one hour's ride brings us to the bridge crossing Kishon, a small, sluggish stream which empties into the Mediterranean Sea near Haifa, the waters of which were once reddened with the blood of the four hundred prophets of Baal whom Elijah slew on the eastern slope of Mount Carmel, at a point near which the river runs.

Passing on to the plain of Acre, as it is called, through which the Kishon runs, and which is so unhealthy that the road over which we have to travel had to be abandoned for a time because the workmen nearly all fell sick of fever, another hour brings us to the hilly region, on the other side of the plain. We take our lunch, in true primitive style, under the shade of a venerable oak, and passing, as we journey onwards, several small villages, at length we reach a large spring, which, at the moment, presents a truly Oriental picture, being surrounded by the dwellers of Nazareth, who come for their supplies of water, the women with water-pots upon their heads, exactly in the style of two thousand years ago, and the men and boys with donkeys carrying each two large jugs, which is no doubt considered a modern innovation. Our craving for a drink of this water, which is said to be excellent, is somewhat abated on seeing several rather untidy-looking women washing dirty clothes on one side of the fountain, while the villagers are filling their vessels with drinking-water from the other side, at a distance of perhaps six feet away. It is highly improbable that the idea has ever entered the heads of any of the frequenters of the spring that there can possibly be any connection between the functions daily performed on the opposite sides; hence we may rationally conclude that their powers of ratiocination are not of a very high order.

Passing on we come, in a few minutes, in sight of the city of Nazareth. The first view in approaching from this direction is disappointing, as we see only a small portion of the place. We soon find ourselves at the door of the Latin Convent, the only place in the city that entertains travellers, where we gain admission and find ourselves in charge of a pale, sickly-looking monk who is to minister to our wants during our visit. Unluckily we find that we have arrived on a fast-day, and before our brief visit is completed we realize that the ordinary bill of fare, which is not luxurious, has been much encroached upon. But no doubt we fare as well as do the monks themselves, although we cease to wonder why they look so pale and puny. We are served with a hearty good-will, and see no sign of greediness or desire to make the most out of us. The monk who waits on us served in the late war, and has two German bullets in his body.

The Latin Monastery stands opposite, and encloses within its high walls the Church of the Annunciation. The building has considerable claims to architectural beauty, and possesses many sacred relics. The principal one is the "House of the Virgin," where she lived with Joseph after the return from Egypt, and where she concealed the young Child during the time Herod was slaughtering the children. It is a kind of cave carved out of rock, beneath the church, and is reached by steps through a dark passage, cut down through the solid rock. Near this room was a smaller one, also subterranean, called the "Kitchen of the Virgin," with a hole at the top for the egress of smoke. The priests are mostly Italians.

Our visit occurred during the service on Sunday morning, and we became much interested in the performance of Mass, which is intoned by the priests, producing in a striking manner the effect of a chime of bells. One bass voice in particular was really grand, being very strong and sonorous, which seemed to form a kind of foundation for all the other voices, as they all rung the changes together, producing the various tones represented by the chimes. The performance serves to produce an effect that will long ring in our ears and live in our memories.

As we stand among the worshippers, listening to these entrancing strains, we are struck with the sharp contrast between the scene before us and that witnessed in a fashionable church in Europe or America. Here there are no pews where the humble are not welcome ; but the humblest and the grandest all mingle in the worship, and are all equal before God. Here is a lesson which may well be copied from the hoary old Roman Catholic Church.

We now visit the old Greek Church, built over the " Well of Mary," a fine Gothic interior, profusely decorated with paintings and containing much old and elaborate carving, also many artistically-painted glass lanterns, silver and cut-glass chandeliers, etc. The well is within the church, and is approached by a flight of stone steps. The attendant priest draws some water in a small silver bucket, and very pure and excellent drinking-water it is. This is the only spring in Nazareth, and the water is conducted in a conduit a considerable distance to a fountain, around which is daily enacted the characteristic scenes which may at any time be witnessed at an Oriental fountain. There can be little doubt that the Virgin Mother and the child Jesus were regular visitors to this spring, and the interest inspired by a visit to the scene now daily transpiring here is greatly increased by the fact that it is very similar to that enacted on the same spot eighteen hundred years ago.

We enjoy very much a visit to the Orphan Asylum for Girls, which is situated near the top of the very high hill back of the town. It seems to be a most admirable institution, planted as it is in the very midst of darkness and misery. The little waifs of humanity are gathered in and taught, and loved, and sustained, thus practically illustrating the sentiment which forms the warp and woof of the utterances and the life of Christ, who lived here and walked these streets nearly thirty years of His life.

The view from the hill back of the asylum is magnificent. To the left in the distance lies the village of Nain, where Christ raised the widow's son. Farther still we trace distinctly the valley of the Jordan, beyond which rise the mountains of Gilead. To the right and far away lies the plain of Esdraelon.

It is now near night and we return to the city to spend one more night in its pestilential atmosphere. We have visited many places that are dirty and malodorous in this country, but Nazareth is the worst of all in this respect. There is no underground drainage, no attempt to organize or observe sanitary laws. All the filth is thrown into the streets, and there it lies festering in the sun's heat, and the entire city smells like a pest-house. The terrible effluvia is everywhere present—indoors and out, night and day.

Our room in the convent faces a kind of square or open place in the principal street in the city, and the picture, as we look out upon it at this moment, is most extraordinary. Some forty or fifty persons, mainly children of both sexes, are clustering round a wagon which has just arrived filled with visitors, who have come to claim the hospitality of the monks. Their garb has all the colors of the rainbow, and more types of style than you could cull from the fashion plates of a hundred years.

The street is, of course, filled with filth, yet no one seems to notice it in the least, and the odors that rise from the seething mass fill all the air; but the natives are blissfully ignorant of all this, and, should this letter fall under their eye, they would, no doubt, roundly abuse me for maligning their beautiful city.

The sidewalk along the convent-yard is occupied by a score or more of native artisans, each with his tools grouped around him as he sits on the pavement. One is making tinware, another repairing old domestic utensils, another making or repairing shoes, etc., etc. Near this group is a street-blacksmith shoeing a refractory mule, just beyond him the barber is pursuing his profession, and so on. All the mechanical appliances and methods are just the same as they were eighteen centuries ago. I have purchased some pocket-knives made by one of these artisans, as he sits on the sidewalk with his rude tools lying around him, which I intend to take to America, and which admirably illustrate the above statement.

An Arab wedding occurred in town the evening of our arrival, and, to the rather characteristic manner they have here of celebrating such an event, we are indebted for two comparatively sleepless nights. The friends of the wedded pair bring to them, for a period of one week, all kinds of food and drink ready prepared for the table, with which they entertain all who call upon them. The couple are thus free from the care of house-keeping for that length of time.

The male friends and relatives parade the streets at night with torches, singing, and firing off guns during a whole week, continuing the din far into and sometimes all night. Last night we were awakened at two o'clock as they passed the convent. The music is very peculiar, being confined to one tone, one group singing and another echoing from a distance, the effect of which is peculiarly weird.

While at Nazareth we make a horseback journey of one hour, by a very rough road over the mountains, to visit "Cana of Galilee." The main point of interest here is the spot where Christ performed the miracle of turning the water into wine at the marriage-feast. A beautiful new church has been built on the spot, with the following inscription over the door; and I have copied the words, as nearly as possible, as they are carved upon the stone:

HIC
CANE
IESUS CHRISTVS
DE AQVA VINVM PROTVLIT.

On our return to Nazareth, as we reach the top of the mountain, we have a magnificent view of the city. We now resume our wagon and return to the sea-coast by the same route as we came.

LETTER IX.

A Visit to Mount Carmel—The Cave of Elijah—Site of the Ancient City of Sycaminum—Rock Caves—Carmelite Monastery—The Mahkraka—Hill of the Priests—A Sacred Grove—A Legend Thereof—At the Druse Village of Dalieh—Some of their Customs—A Primitive Method of Divorce—Ruins of Thirty Cities in Mount Carmel—Honeycombed with Tombs, etc.

Dalieh, January 15, 1886.

PROBABLY there is no place on the surface of the globe fraught with more interest to the student of Scripture history than Mount Carmel, or to which such well-attested traditions of sanctity attach. These traditions come down to us through the various forms of truth and superstition, and cover a period embracing not only the whole of the Christian era, but many centuries of earlier history. It has been a sacred mountain from time immemorial. The traditions respecting the Prophet Elijah seem to be very clear and distinct, and the two extremes of the mountain, which are fourteen miles apart, contain spots which are still held in the highest veneration, as having been the arenas of some of the most remarkable events connected with his career.

The reputed cave of Elijah is situated near the shore of the Mediterranean Sea, and not far from the most western point of Mount Carmel, which here forms an abrupt promontory some five hundred feet in height. It is in the possession of the Roman Catholics. The real cave of Elijah, however, is several hundred feet lower down and near the shore of the sea, and it is frequently visited by Mohammedans, Jews, and Druses, who come to celebrate their observances here by processions and by offering sacrifices of sheep and goats. They often spend the entire night in festivity and dancing, presenting a very picturesque scene when witnessed by the light of their camp-fires. Even the wild Bedouins of the desert often come from beyond the Jordan to join in these sacred rites, the men on their wild steeds, and the women upon camels with their faces concealed.

A short distance to the south of the cave, on a rock plateau projecting into the sea, is a mound said to mark the ancient city of Sycaminum, and the numerous prostrate granite columns and carved marble fragments, capitals, and pedestals scattered around serve to confirm the idea.

Here, too, are found many caves cut out of the solid rock, said, at a remote period, to have been inhabited by hermits, and used, at a later period, by the Crusaders as sentry-boxes. High up above, by an almost perpendicular ascent, stands the Carmelite Monastery, upon an abrupt promontory, and nearly five hundred feet above the level of the sea. The buildings first erected upon this spot seem to have been occupied by monks from the earliest days. Those now standing were erected on the old foundations in 1828, and may be seen at a great distance as the coast is approached from the Mediterranean. The monks are in the habit of accommodating travellers, and reserve a certain number of beds for that purpose.

We now descend to the plain below by a long, shelving road cut into the side of the mountain, at the foot of which we pass the settlement of the German Colony. We propose to make the circuit of the mountain, making note of such points as may seem best calculated to command the popular attention. After leaving the German Colony we pass through the suburbs of Haifa, where we observe a fine grove of palm-trees. They are without branches to the height of sixty or seventy feet. At this point, which is the top of the trunks, the branches, in a cluster, spread out in all directions, and many of them are twenty-five or thirty feet long. As we pass the grove a strong wind is blowing, and the waving of the branches and the sound produced by the wind passing through them is grand indeed.

We skirt the plain of Acre, and about one hour's ride brings us to the village of Sheik, which contains several fine groves of olive-trees. A ride of some two hours from this point, up the precipitous side of the mountain and along its summit, brings us to its eastern terminus, a point of the greatest interest, although very seldom visited by tourists. It seems strange that Mount Carmel, with such a wondrous history, carved deep into its surface, should not be more frequented by travellers, especially as it is so accessible, being immediately on the coast.

On the brow of the mountain, at the extreme eastern end of the Carmel range, is a spot called the Mahkraka (burnt-offering), where Elijah seized the prophets of Baal, after the descent of the fire from heaven in answer to his prayer. From the top of this building, which is sixteen hundred feet above the plain of Esdraelon, we have one of the most magnificent panoramic views to be witnessed anywhere in the world. About fourteen hundred feet below, and almost immediately under our feet, stands the "hill of the priests," where the four hundred false prophets were slain. This hill is situated on the banks of the Kishon; hence this stream is said to have been choked by the carcasses of the slain prophets, and its waters reddened by their blood.

Directly in front and extending far to the right lies the plain of Esdraelon. The valley of the Jordan can be distinctly traced from this point, and the high range of mountains beyond meet the distant horizon. In the same direction we see Nazareth and Safed, Mt. Tabor, Little Hermon, Mt. Gilboa, and Mt. Gilead. Further to the right lie Galilee and Samaria. To the left lies the city of Acre, with its beautiful bay, and in the distance double-peaked Mt. Hermon, covered with its mantle of white. We gain a view here of almost every point of note in Galilee.

We turn our faces westward, and as our horses, well used to these rough paths, pass on through the valleys and over the mountain-tops we find many points of interest. To the right is a cluster of forty large trees, which is regarded as a sacred grove. The legend concerning them is that forty Moslem sheiks were massacred here, and that these forty trees were planted to commemorate the event, and that any one who should attempt to cut them down would forfeit his life. It is said that two men, father and son, undertook to fell one of them, and both died on the spot.

We see in passing many Arab shepherds, with their variegated and tattered garb and bare legs; for the mountain is the pasture-ground for all their animals. Many camels are thus pastured when not in use bearing their burdens. During this trip along the top of the Carmel range we passed several encampments of Bedouin Arabs, with their black camels. They group their tents in larger or smaller numbers, according as they find pasturage for their animals, abundant or otherwise, at the spot selected. In some parts of our journey we followed the paths that have been used for centuries, and in many places the feet of the animals have cut a narrow track out of the solid stone from six to ten feet deep.

Being on the very back-bone of the mountain, we look down, at many points sixteen hundred or seventeen hundred feet, upon the plain through which the sluggish Kishon winds its way to the sea, and across to the mountains of northern Galilee. To-day it is so clear that we can plainly see several snow-capped summits of the Lebanon range far beyond Mount Hermon, which is at least eighty miles away. The bay of Acre, with its graceful curve, lies almost at our feet, and the broad Mediterranean stretches far away to the distant horizon, with no prow ploughing its bosom and no sail whitening its surface as we look.

We now arrive at the Druse village of Dalieh. Some two hundred and fifty years ago the famous warrior Fahkr-ed-Deen planted his first Druse settlement here, and at one period they numbered four thousand in Carmel. Only two villages remain of the eight formerly here—Dalieh and Esfia -containing together about eight hundred people. The Druses have many singular customs. They observe great secrecy in their religious rites, and never tolerate the presence of a stranger in their place of worship. Hence little is known of their religious belief and practices. They are subjected to many cruel exactions and merciless persecutions by the Turkish government, and seem to be powerless to defend themselves against their Moslem neighbors. Their persecutions have, no doubt, made them amiable, for they are said to be a much more agreeable people to live among than either the Christians or Mohammedans.

In company with a gentleman who resides at Haifa, and who has a summer residence near Dalieh, I made a visit to the spiritual sheik. His house is built of stone, with a solid stone floor, and has but two apartments—one for the family and one for the animals, all under one roof and in close proximity. As their flocks and herds are large, and the room in this part of the house is limited, only the more domestic animals are sheltered here. As this is a genuine Eastern house, it affords an excellent idea of the kind of place in which Christ was born.

We are received with great dignity and made most welcome. As the only article of furniture in the house is the rug which is spread upon the floor for us to sit upon, we proceed to occupy it with all the grace and dignity we can command, with the full consciousness that we cannot vie with our host in this regard, as he assumes the same position upon the floor in front of us. With true politeness he strives to make us feel at our ease, and, after a brief interview (my friend could converse with him in Arabic), during which Turkish coffee is served in delicate little cups, we begin to feel quite Oriental. Later in the day our host returns the call at the residence of my friend, who seats himself on the floor with his guest while the coffee is served, thus relieving him from the embarrassment of attempting to sit in a European chair.

The Druse religion is said by their enemies to allow certain gross immoralities and cruel practices; but they keep everything so secret that little can be known except what may be inferred from their outward lives and manners.

We are forcibly struck with the evidences we see on every hand that this mountain was once thickly populated, and it is supposed that the range at one time contained fifty thousand people. My friend, who has had large experience in making explorations, has already discovered the ruins of thirty cities in Mount Carmel, many of them very extensive, and the ground may almost be said to be honeycombed with tombs and water-cisterns. In making the excavations for the foundations of his house at Dalieh the workmen came upon the wall of an ancient structure, and, after the house was completed and a small elevation was being removed to level the ground around it, he discovered the mouth of a cistern which was filled with débris. As it was located just where he required a cistern for rain-water, he had it cleared of the rubbish (hundreds of loads were taken out), and the result was an immense cistern, excavated from solid rock, and in every way adapted to his purpose.

As Dalieh is situated at the head of a valley leading to the base of the mountain, we pass down by a well-trodden path and reach the shore of the Mediterranean at Athlit, an extensive ruin, celebrated as the last stronghold surrendered by the Crusaders, and after a ride of five miles reach the village of Tareh, which is inhabited by a band of turbulent and predatory Moslems, who are the terror of their neighbors, and especially of the Druses. They have appropriated most of their lands by force. During the last few years, however, they have been less troublesome than formerly, the increasing population and advancing civilization of the neighborhood having essentially curbed their predatory instincts.

Proceeding northward, one hour's ride brings us to the promontory crowned by the convent, thus completing the circuit of the mountain.

LETTER X.

Haifa and Acre—Delightful Winter Weather—Cheap Fruit—The Olive Crop—The Features of Haifa—Enterprise of its German Colony—Their Persecutions—Monumental Manure-Heaps—Acre, One of the Oldest Cities in the World—Besieged Seventeen Times—The Rivers Kishon and Belus—Discovery of Glass—Jezzar, the Butcher Pasha of Acre, etc., etc.

HAIFA, January 20, 1885.

AS we are about to take leave of this wonderful historic land, our last word shall be from Haifa and Acre, which are situated on opposite sides of the beautiful bay of Acre, from which we are to embark in a few days on our long journey homeward. Doubtless you are, in America, in the midst of winter at this moment. This is what they call winter here, too, but it has none of the characteristics of our northern winters. The mercury ranges from fifty-five to seventy degrees, and within the last two weeks, since the rains commenced, the fields are clothed in green. The farmers are ploughing and sowing their seed, and we have, in fact, a duplicate of our most beautiful spring weather. Fresh vegetables are abundant and very cheap, and the orange-trees are loaded with their luscious fruit. Within one rod of the door we pick from the trees our before-breakfast oranges.

Fruits are very cheap here. Passing through the market a few days ago, as we were starting on an excursion, we purchased thirteen splendid oranges for one piastre—less than four cents. A like sum of money will purchase enough bunches of crisp radishes to fill a half-bushel measure. Some of these grow to an enormous size—as large as a quart wine bottle.

The principal crop is grain, immense quantities of which are brought to the coast on camels and donkeys, for shipment. The principal fruits are oranges, lemons, grapes, figs, and olives, all of which are largely exported. There are many very extensive olive-groves. I have seen several, which were planted by the Crusaders during the eleventh and twelfth centuries, which are still bearing fruit, though six or seven hundred years old. Some of these old trees have gradually rotted away on the inside, leaving the outside of the trunk in distinct parts, looking almost like a group of trees, the branches above still bearing fruit.

The olive crop is rather uncertain on account

of the sirocco, which sometimes prevails just as the buds are forming, and totally ruins the crop. Exactly this happened last year, and there was no olive-oil made. Hence the Arabs and others who make the oil usually keep on hand a year's supply to meet such a contingency. The oil produced by the Arabs is of poor quality, as they are careless in their methods. A limited quantity of superior quality is made in this vicinity, which is nearly all sent to America, and which is much sought for there, as it is beyond question pure olive-oil; and those who understand the facts best know how difficult it is to get in the market an oil that is not adulterated either with cotton-seed or some other vegetable substance. Indeed, the adulteration of this article has become so almost universal that dealers say that if they could give their customers a pure article they would object to it because it did not taste like that they have become accustomed to.

The exact site of the old town of Haifa is somewhat involved in doubt. It is supposed to be identical with ancient Sycaminum, which is mentioned by ancient Greek and Roman authors, the ruins of which are located some two miles from the present town, which dates from the middle of the eighteenth century. Haifa possesses considerable importance as a seaport town, and is regularly visited by the steamers of the Austrian-Lloyds line. It is located immediately at the foot of Mount Carmel, on a narrow plateau, which increases considerably in width towards the point on which the mountain is located.

One of the most noteworthy and interesting features of Haifa is the settlement here of a group of Germans, known as the German Colony. They came here some twenty-five years ago, being prompted to emigrate thither by a religious sentiment. There are three distinct colonies of them in Palestine—at Jerusalem, Jaffa, and Haifa—consisting of about one thousand members. The colony here numbers some three hundred persons, and they are in many respects a remarkable people. The appearance of the part of the city they occupy is in striking contrast with the main town in that it is regularly laid out, and is clean and orderly. These colonists are the only people who have ever come to live in Palestine who are self-supporting. All others live upon the means they bring with them; but the colonists, though they brought money with them at first, and have it invested in lands and different industries, now make their living in the country, and are slowly gaining. They labor under great difficulties, as the Turkish government is very hostile to them, as it is to everybody who tries to introduce any kind of improvement into the country. The Carmelite monks, too, whose lands join theirs, are envious, jealous, and hostile towards them, and annoy them in all possible ways.

They are engaged in persecuting the colonists at this moment, having by bribery procured an order from the local Turkish official, posting a soldier in a position on their grounds, whereby he becomes a serious annoyance to them. But with admirable patience, and with wonderful persistence and wisdom, they work their way through all difficulties, and their example is having a marked effect upon the neighborhood. Some ten years ago they built, at their own expense, a tolerable wagon-road to Nazareth, a distance of twenty-two miles, and since they settled here have done a number of such things, introducing many improvements which serve to benefit the community as well as themselves.

A good story is related of them, which illustrates their thrift and the want of that element on the part of the natives here. It has been for centuries the custom of the people of this country to deposit the manure at the edge of their town in a large pile, and it is no exaggeration whatever to state that the manure-heap in many of their towns is much the most imposing structure they can boast of, for it is the accretion of centuries. When the colonists first settled here they attacked the manure-heap and carried it all away in the course of the two years and spread it upon their lands. The natives watched them with curious interest, but did not take the hint till they carried it all away. When, however, they saw the wonderful crops the colonists gathered, they wanted manure too, but were too late. They do not now deposit it as formerly, nor do the colonists get it. But, strange to say, so obtuse are the people of this country, and so slowly does the news travel, that a knowledge of the above facts has not penetrated ten miles into the interior. On our recent journey to Nazareth we saw, in towns we passed, the traditional pile of manure. In many cases, too, it was perfectly evident that the lands immediately adjoining were suffering for the want of the very material that was so near that it could be thrown upon it with a shovel.

We will now make a circuit of the bay and pay

a visit to Acre, one of the oldest cities in the world, and the theatre of more extraordinary and startling events than any place of which we have a well-defined record. Leaving the beautiful city of palms to our right, we find a hard and perfectly smooth road directly on the beach the entire distance.

About two miles from Haifa we come to the mouth of the Kishon, which we recognize at once by its pestilential odors. Although this is the second river in magnitude in Palestine (the Jordan only being larger), during most of the dry seasons it discharges no water into the sea, the mouth being blocked by a bank of sand, and the water formed into pools and lagoons on the plain above, thus rendering the neighborhood unhealthy.

Much of the way the shore is thickly strewn with small shells. From one species of these the Phœnicians in ancient times used to extract the famous Tyrian purple, a very minute quantity of which was found in a small vessel in the throat of the fish inhabiting the shell. These prickly shells are still found in limited numbers, and are very beautiful. Just before we reach Acre we cross the mouth of a small river called the Belus. It was at this point, on the shores of the river, that glass was first discovered. Some Roman soldiers encamped here observed that the sea-sand under their camp-fires vitrified, and from this arose the manufacture of glass.

Seventeen different sieges of Acre are easily traced, beginning with Thotmes, who invaded Palestine from Egypt three hundred years before Moses led the Israelites into Canaan. The most bloody on record are those of the Crusaders, in one of which sixty thousand Christians perished. In the early part of this century it was besieged by Napoleon, whose army was driven back by the English fleet, under Sir Sidney Smith, upon which occasion the magazine blew up and eighteen hundred people perished. The last siege was by the English fleet under Sir Charles Napier, during the occupation of the country by the Egyptians, who had conquered it, and whose victorious progress was then crushed, and the country was given back by the English to the Sultan of Turkey. It was on this occasion that Sir Charles Napier is said to have used the memorable expression to his sailors, when they landed as a storming party: "Now land, you beggars, and fulfil prophecy."

At the time of the invasion of Palestine by the Egyptians under Ibrahim Pasha, Acre had been governed by the descendants of a pasha who had thrown off the Turkish rule and exercised an independent authority. The most celebrated of these was Jezzar, appropriately named the butcher, whose career of unprecedented cruelty is said to have originated in the following incident: One day as he held his little daughter in his lap, and she was stroking his beard with her hand, he said to her: "Why do you stroke my beard?" She replied: "That is the way my mother does to the mamelukes." This roused his suspicion, and he soon gave out word that he was going on a journey, but he returned suddenly late the same night and found the mamelukes in the harem enjoying themselves with his wives; whereupon he slew with his own sword fifteen of them on the spot, and had every mameluke in his employ and the entire harem put to death at once.

After this to the end of his life he proved to be one of the most bloodthirsty wretches that ever lived. It is related that he took special delight in putting out the eyes and cutting off the noses of any of his favorites who incurred his displeasure. He built the mosque and other structures of materials brought from ruins in different parts of Palestine. The pillars of the mosque he procured at Cæsarea, and most of the stone from the ruins of Athlit. The grounds around the mosque are especially harmonious and beautiful, one of the most marked features being the blending of stately palm-trees with numerous of these columns, which are used to support the fountain and other structures adjoining the mosque. Jezzar Pasha also built the water-works and the aqueduct from the distant mountains, which still supplies the city with excellent water. His tomb is in the enclosure of the mosque.

From the first Egyptian siege under Thothmes to the last under Sir Charles Napier, forty-five years ago, Acre has been considered the strategetic key to Palestine. The dilapidated condition of the fortress and the modern inventions of military science have deprived it of this character, and it would offer no serious obstacle at the present day to an invading army.

The area within the city walls is only about fifty acres, on which nine thousand people are hived, and a large part of this space is occupied by mosques, old towers and walls, public buildings, plazas, etc., leaving one to greatly wonder where so many people can be stowed away, or how they can possibly live in so crowded and filthy a place.

We now return to Haifa, and as we reach the portion of the place occupied by the German Colony we are more than ever struck with the sharp contrast between these Germans and the natives of the country. "As we look at this tidy village, transplanted, as it were, from Europe to the foot of Mount Carmel, and mark the signs of modern husbandry upon its long neglected slopes, it seems as though the first step in its regeneration is already taken, and that the dawn of a better period may at last be breaking after its lonely night of desolation and gloom."

LETTER XI.

Leaving Haifa—Homeward Bound—Stopping on the Way—At Port Said—Poor Steamers and Worse Accommodations—Ismailïa—An Old and Handsomely Laid Out Town—Cairo, the Largest City in Africa—Street Scenes—The Khedive's and Other Official Residences—The Pyramids of Gizeh—Road Leading Thereto—The Great Pyramid of Cheops—The Sphinx—Old Cairo—Church of St. Mary—The Most Ancient Mosque in Egypt—The Island of Rhodda—Its Nileometer—The Citadel—Superb Mosque—An Obelisk—Ostrich Farm—Chateau of Gezireh, etc., etc.

CAIRO, January 25, 1886.

AFTER spending six weeks in Palestine, and visiting many places rendered notable by the important events connected with their history, of which I have endeavored to give some passing description that might serve as a kind of pen-and-ink substitute for an actual visit to them, I now turn my face homeward. As the journey will be somewhat deliberately executed, if I have succeeded in interesting my readers in the places already described they may perhaps be glad to visit with me some others on the homeward journey.

Leaving Haifa on the small Austrian steamer

which touches there only twice a month, we are two days making the distance of some one hundred and thirty miles, as they stop at Jaffa all night at anchor, and, indeed, all the next day, and so arrive in Port Said the second day. Here it was as warm as summer almost. There is little of interest here for the traveller, as it is a recently built city, which has, in fact, sprung into existence since the opening of the great canal across the isthmus of Suez, which was completed in 1869. It is situated at the northern extremity of the Suez Canal, and has a harbor of about six hundred acres, which was excavated by dredging to the depth of twenty-six feet. Large and small steamers, bound to and from India, are constantly arriving and departing. There is comparatively little business done here except that connected with shipping. Almost every other building is the office of some steamship line.

There is a line of small steamboats which carry the mails daily between Port Said and Ismailia. In one of these we embark at twelve o'clock at night. It is about the size and shape of a canal-boat, and forcibly reminds me of a trip made thirty-seven years ago from Harrisburg to Pittsburgh, in Pennsylvania, when the first-class passenger trade was carried on by those canal packets; and they were certainly much more comfortable than these steam canal packets. During the daytime we had the whole space the entire length of the boat (except a small space for the kitchen), and at night this was changed into a sleeping apartment, with comfortable berths put up at the sides. In these Egyptian boats there are no berths, and only a very small room in one end of the boat for passengers, about eight feet by twelve, where all are crowded in together to spend the night as best they can. Of course it is neither clean nor well ventilated, and we have to pay dear for coming this way to see the Suez Canal, not only in the price of the fare, but in the discomforts to be encountered.

By six o'clock the next morning we compass the journey of thirty-five miles, and arrive at that most uncomfortable hour at Ismailïa. This is an old town, and is very handsomely laid out, and, as it is located on the railroad from Suez to Cairo, we breakfast here and leave at noon for the latter place. We are glad to see a railroad train once more, even though we do find this rather a poor specimen of a road. We are six hours in going the seventy miles to Cairo. The whole equipment seems to be made up of the played-out rolling stock of some English railroad. For the first forty miles the road leads through a desert, there being no vegetation whatsoever; but as we approach Cairo all becomes green and luxuriant, as we are now in the valley of the Nile, which here seems about twenty miles wide and is everywhere irrigated during the dry season. The soil is deep and rich, as black and fertile as that of our Western prairies, quite like what we call our rich bottom lands in the West.

Cairo is much the largest city on the continent of Africa, having a population of some 400,000. It is unquestionably one of the oldest cities in the world. It had so large a population in the eleventh century that 900,000 of its inhabitants were swept away with the plague in the course of a few months. The present population is made up of a most extraordinary combination of nationalities, rendering it more cosmopolitan, if possible, than even Constantinople.

Among the most interesting features here are the street scenes, which are exceedingly unique and varied, and furnish a source of never-ending amusement to the denizen of western civilization, unaccustomed as he is to Oriental scenes

and manners. There is scarcely anything one
sees in the East more calculated to make a lasting
impression than these scenes daily enacted
in the streets of Cairo. By using a carriage for
visiting all parts of the city we especially enjoy
these scenes as we wind our way through the
noisy throngs. A very prominent factor in the
crowd are the beggars of various grades. They
all agree in one quality—persistence. No rebuff
or any number of them discourages them in the
least.

The two parts of the city are distinguished as
Cairo and Old Cairo. The more modern part
is well laid out, and many portions of it are well
built, having a clean and comfortable appearance.
Many large and substantial villas are seen, situated
in the midst of extensive gardens filled with
trees and shrubbery, while here and there the
noble palm-tree presides over the surrounding
scene with stately dignity.

The residences of the Khedive and other dignitaries,
scattered through the city, occupy with
their extensive grounds a large amount of space,
each surrounded by its high wall of solid masonry.
But there is no lack of room, for there
seems to be plenty of unoccupied land within
the city limits, which, however, is being gradu-

ally filled with new buildings, all of which are built in a substantial manner of stone, and many of them with considerable pretensions to architectural beauty.

Let me attempt a brief account of some of the principal points of interest visited. First, the pyramids of Gizeh, which are reached by a carriage ride of ten miles on a wide road elevated about twelve feet above the level of the fields, which are all overflowed by the waters of the Nile once a year. This road was constructed by the government and contains two rows of beautiful shade-trees, leaving a charming shaded drive in the centre the entire distance from the city to the pyramids. Before entering on this road we cross the Nile on a substantial iron bridge, which seems to be of recent construction.

At the end of this avenue the pyramids are approached by a rapid ascent, and as they stand about one hundred feet above the surrounding plain the view where the road begins the ascent is very imposing. But on a near approach the impression is disappointing. They have an exceedingly rough and unfinished appearance, and are constructed of large stones of irregular shapes and sizes ; and in many places the stones are crumbling away. Several layers must have been removed from the top of the principal pyramid, as it does not come to a point, but has a flat space of several feet square, from which those who take the trouble to climb up must have a magnificent view. It is said to have been built by Cheops, one of the kings of Egypt, who reigned fifty years. Over 100,000 of his subjects were engaged parts of each year for some thirty years in quarrying and transporting the stones, and building the pyramid, which was intended for his tomb. It is said that he built a small monument in the pyramid shape, and after it was completed added another layer, then another, till the present structure was the result; and it is presumed that if his reign had extended beyond the fifty years he would have kept on still adding other layers, and so increasing its size. This, the largest one of the group, occupies nearly thirteen acres of ground, and is one mass of solid stone, except a very limited space taken up by interior rooms, probably used as tombs for the builder and his family.

The brother of Cheops, who succeeded him on the throne, built the next pyramid in size, during the fifty-five years of his reign, and it seems to have become the custom of each king, for a long time subsequently, to build a pyramid for his tomb. Hence the large number of them that are standing to-day.

The Sphinx is a colossal, rude stone lion with the head of a man. It was built in a crouching position with the immense head towering high in the air. The face is much mutilated. The nose is said to have been shot off by the mamelukes, who used it as a target, and the face is otherwise damaged. This group of monuments must for ever remain a comparative enigma to the visitor, after all that is known of them from history and tradition, and no doubt hundreds of generations of our future brothers will gaze upon them, as we do, with wonder and delight.

Returning to the city we are just in season to meet the surging crowd of carriages, pedestrians, camels, donkeys, etc., that cross the bridge on the closing of the draw, which is daily opened for an hour at two P.M. Turning to the right, a short ride brings us to Old Cairo, with its narrow, dirty streets and quaint architecture.

We visit the old Coptic Church of St. Mary, in the cave of which it is claimed that the Virgin and Child spent a month after their flight from Palestine. The Copts here celebrate many religious festivals, such as Palm Sunday, the anniversary of the baptism of Christ, and others.

We next come to the most ancient mosque in Egypt, the Gam-a-Amr, which is some five hundred feet square, with a large, open court in the middle, each of the four sides consisting of a series of high arches supported by numerous columns, the whole being covered with a roof. There were originally three hundred and sixty of these columns; but many of them have fallen, and some still lie on the ground, while others have been carried away. The appearance of the mosque would indicate that the claim to antiquity is a legitimate one.

This old part of Cairo was once the centre of the immense population, though now it is merely a suburb of the city. Opposite this section of the city is the island of Rhodda, which we reach by a ferry across the arm of the Nile. The principal object of interest here is the Nileometer, a column in the middle of a wide well which is connected with the Nile. On the column are engraved figures to indicate the height of the water, and at the period of the annual overflow the Nileometer is watched with all-absorbing interest.

On a commanding height, quite on the other side of the city, is situated a large structure known as the Citadel, from which a grand view of Cairo is obtained. It is in the hands of the English, and filled with British soldiers. Every part of the city can be readily reached by their guns.

In an inner court of the Citadel we come to the Mosque of Mohammed Ali. It is called the Alabaster Mosque, the pillars and the interior walls being made of that material, presenting a most ornamental and rich appearance. The centre dome is very high and the whole interior exceedingly imposing.

In leaving the Citadel we pass the finest specimen of Arabian architecture in existence, the Mosque of the Sallan Hassan, known as the "Superb Mosque." It is very high, and portions of the dome are covered with a peculiar kind of ornamented wood-work, which appears like black walnut, and which is gradually dropping off, as it is apparently never repaired. It is at least eighty feet from the pavement, and has the appearance of having been untouched for centuries.

After a ride of some eight miles from the city, nearly in an easterly direction, through another of the shaded avenues for which Cairo is famous, to visit one of the oldest obelisks of Egypt, all that remains of the ancient Heliopolis. It consists of a single stone, sixty-six feet high and six feet square at the base, covered with hieroglyphics, which tell its story. Its companion obelisk was destroyed in A.D. 656.

Returning to the city, we visit, on the way, the celebrated ostrich farm, where the birds are hatched by steam-heat. We saw some two hundred of the birds, from the tiny infant of five weeks to the full-grown ostrich of eight years, standing fully eight feet high. The plumage of some of the larger birds was very beautiful.

About two miles down the Nile, and opposite Cairo, stands the Chateau of Gezireh, the former residence of the ex-Khedive, who is an exile from his country and is living at Naples, Italy. It is untenanted, and looks lonesome in all its magnificence of furniture and artistic work.

There are a great many points of interest that might be worth mentioning but my limits forbid —the tombs of the Mamelukes, tombs of the Caliphs, the bazaars, the Monastery of the Dervishes, the Museum of Egyptian Antiquities, etc. The latter is one of the most interesting places in Cairo, as it has a large collection of statuary, tombs, and mummies, with a great variety of gold ornaments found in the tombs, in some cases amounting to thousands of dollars in value in a single tomb. No traveller should omit a visit here, as it is a kind of epitome of Egypt, and shows one as much as he could see in travelling thousands of miles.

This is the height of the season in Egypt, and all the hotels are crowded with tourists. Parties are almost daily departing for the upper Nile. We meet many Americans, also large numbers of Englishmen, and many Germans.

LETTER XII.

From Cairo to Alexandria—The Valley of the Nile—How the Land is Irrigated—Different Methods of Raising the Water—The Wonderful Land of Egypt—Alexandria—A Visit to Pompey's Pillar—The Catacombs—Leaving Alexandria—Review of, and Reflections Upon, the Journey thus far—Valuable Things Learned about Business, Eating, etc.—Some Advice—Messina in Sicily.

MESSINA, January 30, 1886.

WE leave Cairo and run the distance to Alexandria, one hundred and thirty miles, in about five hours—good speed for this part of the world. The route lies the entire distance through the valley of the Nile, and it is almost a dead level. On the way we see many marks of the peculiar civilization obtaining here, and are especially impressed by the way they manage the water, which everywhere premeates the country from the Nile. They evidently depend upon this water for their crops, for there is scarcely any rain here at any season. By the annual overflow of the Nile the ground is thoroughly soaked for some three or four weeks, and the numerous canals and irrigating ditches are filled for future use. Many of the canals lead the water from the Nile at its ordinary stage, and it is then lifted into the irrigating ditches by various curious appliances. The usual way is by a kind of wheel constructed upon the principle of a grain elevator. The wheel is of large diameter, and in some cases the water is lifted by chambers or buckets, which are filled when they are submerged and emptied as they rise to the top by the revolution of the wheel. Many of the wheels have a series of earthen jars tied on the centre of the rim, which are filled and emptied in the same manner. The power is furnished by an ox or buffalo, which plods its weary round all day long. This is, no doubt, one of the oldest mechanical appliances to be found in the country, and, from the present appearance of the many samples we have seen, no improvements have been added for thousands of years.

We observe a still more extraordinary method of elevating the water which is employed at points where the wheels had not been set up. It is by means of a basket hung in the middle of a long rope, which two men handle from its ends. They plunge the basket into the water by a peculiarly dexterous motion and fill it, and then by a swinging lift raise it and pour the water into the basin that conducts it away into the ditch. Although it is raised very quickly, it is evident that a considerable portion of the water leaks out before it can be emptied; and it is highly probable, too, that this process has been going on some thousands of years, and no ingenious Egyptian has ever thought of lining the basket so that it would hold water.

We have also seen during our trip to-day thousands of old-fashioned well-sweeps in constant motion raising the water by buckets for the same purpose. It reminded us of our childhood days, when we used to drink from "the old oaken bucket" which was raised in this manner by the old well-sweep from the cool depths beneath. The fertility of the soil in the valley of the Nile is something wonderful, and is attributable mainly to the deposit made on the surface by the annual overflow.

Egypt is the arena of some of the principal events recorded in Bible history, both of the Old and the New Testaments. The earliest of these is the journey of Abraham into Egypt at the time of the great famine, and out of which event grew the wonderful history of Joseph, perhaps the most fascinating story recounted in the Old Testament.

We are now at Alexandria, a city of over two hundred thousand inhabitants, situated at the principal mouth of the Nile. There is a saying that to the traveller approaching it from Europe it appears quite like an Eastern city, but to one coming from the East it appears quite European in its aspect. The latter is certainly true, for the contrast between this beautiful city and the best built cities we saw in Palestine is very marked. The streets are wide, and there are many splendid blocks four and five stories high, and many fine private residences.

The one special thing worthy of a visit is Pompey's Pillar. This is a grand shaft of red granite, beautifully polished, and, as it stands upon an eminence on the edge of the city, it presents a very commanding appearance. The whole monument is one hundred feet high. It consists of a single shaft upon a base of about sixteen feet high, with a cap at the summit which is crumbling away with age. The cap and base both appear to be of inferior material and workmanship. The absence of the statue that once adorned its summit detracts much from its symmetry and beauty. But there it stands connecting the centuries, stretching far back into the dim distance, with the present period of busy and bustling activities.

We close our visit to Alexandria with a view of the catacombs, the fortifications, and the bazaar, and a ride through the suburbs, and prepare ourselves to embark once more on the Mediterranean in the pursuance of our long journey homeward.

The harbor of Alexandria is large, and is protected by a long mole constructed of large blocks of artificial stone, made of a combination of cement, sand, etc. Large war-vessels of the French, English, Italian, and Turkish fleets, also the khedive's steam-yacht, lie at anchor in the harbor, and many steamers are loading and discharging, besides a large number of sailing-vessels, presenting altogether a very busy scene. The position of Alexandria makes it a port of increasing importance, lying as it does directly in the route from England to the East, via the Suez Canal.

We are now leaving Alexandria by one of the vessels of the Florio-Rubatino line, the principal Italian line of steamers in the Mediterranean. Our vessel has just had a new engine put in, and some friction of the parts is causing us serious delay, giving us ample time for a mental review of our journey thus far, and for any suggestions that may be prompted thereby. To visit different countries and witness the various habits of life, social customs, and religious beliefs and practices can have no other than a broadening influence upon the traveller, especially if he endeavors to divest himself of the prejudices he may naturally entertain concerning the social customs and religious beliefs prevailing in his own country. Extensive travelling in other countries than one's own is very apt to convince him that his own country can claim no monopoly of the best things obtainable in this life.

In contrasting our own country with others, especially with reference to inventions and improvements in the appliances of our domestic and manufacturing processes, we cannot fail to see a great difference in our favor, yet in many other respects we may learn valuable lessons from our neighbors. In the matter of religion we may at least learn the great lesson of toleration. We see others as earnest and sincere in their beliefs and conviction as we can be. Indeed, the wild Arab of the desert will often put to shame the Christian, who looks upon him with pity, by the earnestness and fervor of his devotions. If by contrast with the believers in other religions than our own we learn to *keep silent*, and let the influence of our religion upon our own lives constitute the only proselyting agency in our association with others, we learn the greatest lesson of all.

But there are two things which we may learn of European and Eastern nations that would be a great improvement upon our present methods and tend much to improve our health and comfort, and these are our methods of business and our habits of eating. We find nowhere away from our own country the terrible rush and incessant strain that everywhere prevail among our business men. To make money is not everywhere the sole object of life, as it appears to be with us; but the enjoyment of life, social claims, and amusement have a much larger share of the time and attention of the business man, and this reacts upon him, conferring health and vigor and longer life.

In like manner the habits of eating in these countries are a vast improvement upon ours. Instead of dining with railroad speed upon two or three dishes and drinking a quantity of ice-water, the dinner here is a deliberate affair, consisting of a series of dishes, which are partaken of deliberately, and a light, tart wine is the universal dinner beverage. For instance, our dinner on this steamer last night consisted of eleven courses, the plates being changed for each course, and we were an hour and a half at table. Excellent Italian red wine in abundance is furnished free to each first-class passenger. I have noticed that our national disease, the dyspepsia, is almost unknown in these Eastern countries, where overeating and fast eating do not prevail as with us. There can be little doubt that the great prevalence of dyspepsia in the United States arises mostly from the nervous excitement produced by overwork, and from rapid eating and consequent overeating.

It is curious and interesting to notice the different customs and hours of meals. On the Atlantic steamers they serve a substantial meat breakfast at eight, a lunch, about equal to a dinner, except the soup, at one, a dinner at six, and a hearty supper at nine; while on the steamers in the Mediterranean they serve a small cup of coffee, with a small, dry cracker only, on rising; at ten a breakfast of four or five courses, with wine; and at five P.M. an elaborate dinner, and at nine a cup of tea. Stopping with a friend in London, on the journey out, we had a delicate breakfast at eight, dinner at one, tea at five, and a hearty supper at nine, with porter, ale, and wine. While in Palestine, being again a guest in a private family, we took breakfast at eight, lunch at twelve, tea at three, dinner at seven, and tea again at nine. But every meal, at whatever the hour, is taken with great deliberation. Perhaps our readers may think that these details are not interesting, but I note them because it is quite evident that we Americans need "line upon line" on this subject.

After four days' sailing, the mountainous and highly picturesque coast of Calabria, the southernmost point of Italy, meets our welcome gaze to the right, and at the same moment the most perfect rainbow I have ever witnessed spans the entire circuit from horizon to horizon. It is raining for the moment on the mountains, and the picture presented is exceedingly grand and gorgeous; the high mountains, with their fertile valleys studded with villas, in the background, the rain and mist partly concealing them, and the brilliant rainbow standing out with its unrivalled colors in front, while there is a distinct reflection of the rainbow on the sea between our vessel and the shore.

A few minutes more and we discern a high range of mountains on the left, disclosing to our view the coast of Sicily, and an hour more brings us to Messina, the most important commercial city in Sicily. It is grandly located, having the high mountains of Sicily in the immediate background, and across the Straits of Messina the Calabrian range. The city is said to have been founded by pirates in the eighth century, and it has passed through many vicissitudes caused by wars and revolutions, as well as by earthquakes, pestilence, etc. It has a population of some 75,000, and is at present in a flourishing condition, arising largely from its favorable location for commerce.

Leaving Messina, twenty hours more will bring us into Naples, the beauty of whose famed bay has been praised by so many eloquent tongues and pens.

LETTER XIII.

Leaving Messina—The Volcano of Stromboli—Bay of Naples—How it Compares with New York Bay—The City of Naples—A Visit to Pompeii—Description of the Houses—The Temples, Theatres, and Basilicas—Herculaneum—The Museum and its Statuary from the Buried Cities—Palaces, Catacombs, and Tombs — A Ride through Naples — An Eruption of Mount Vesuvius.

NAPLES, February 5, 1886.

LEAVING Messina at eight P.M., we are soon again ploughing the rough surface of the Mediterranean. We pass the island of Stromboli at one o'clock, but our midnight vigil is only rewarded by a slight curl of smoke issuing from the crater of the volcano bearing the same name. We well remember the description of the volcano of Stromboli in the geography of our school-boy days, and as we are now to pass within two or three miles of its base we determine to sit up and make its more intimate acquaintance, fondly hoping for some fitful gleam at least, if not a grand pyrotechnic display, from its cloud-capped crater. But the internal forces seem disinclined to favor us, as they evidently lie slumbering far down in the depths below, slowly accreting, no doubt, the power which, on some more fortunate day, will burst suddenly forth, thus affording other travellers the grand view we so much crave, and so freshly illustrating the oft-noted fact that real or fancied good often eludes the grasp of those who most earnestly crave it, while it comes unexpectedly to those who least anticipate it.

The sea at this point of our journey is giving us a lively dance, in which the chairs, table, and breakfast dishes join. But we are approaching the famed bay of Naples. In the early morning we pass the precipitous rocks which constitute the island of Capri, and so enter the bay, and we soon find that no description, however eloquent, can convey an adequate conception of its beauty and grandeur. It is immensely large and the water is evidently deep, with no obstructions to navigation. It is twelve miles long, from the island of Capri to Naples, and some ten miles wide. When Jenny Lind sailed up the bay of New York for the first time, on a beautiful day, standing upon the deck of the steamer, she declared to Mr. Barnum, who stood beside her, that its beauties fully equalled those of the bay of Naples, and that she had never witnessed a more beautiful scene. If any apology were needed for such an opinion from the famed songstress, it might be found in the enthusiasm of the occasion. She might naturally desire to place herself on a good footing with the citizens of a great nation, who were soon to welcome her so warmly and praise and admire her so enthusiastically.

The bay of New York is as beautiful as the bay of Naples, but the latter is much larger, and is partially surrounded by very high and commanding mountains; and Mount Vesuvius, towering so high as to be covered, in this low latitude, with snow nearly half way down to its base, adds a feature of great beauty at all times, and more especially during the periods of eruption.

But New York, if her harbor is smaller and more difficult of access, has made a better use of her facilities than Naples. The commerce of the latter is comparatively insignificant. There are only some half a dozen steamers and a score or two of sailing vessels in port at present, and they all lie snugly clustered together in a small inner harbor, thus leaving the immense expanse of the great harbor with rather a deserted and lonesome aspect. As you enter the city of Naples you fail to recognize the vigorous throbs of that mighty commerce which quickens the heartbeats of the great commercial emporium of the western continent.

Considering the fact that Naples is by far the largest city in Italy, having some 600,000 inhabitants, the aspect of its streets and buildings is disappointing, and there is also a comparative dearth of the famous works of art that one expects to find on visiting Italy. The valuable treasures of antiquity that have been exhumed from Herculaneum and Pompeii are by far the most important to be found here, and serve, in some degree, to compensate for the lack of works of superior merit.

Naples dates back more than one thousand years before Christ, and until several centuries of the Christian era had elapsed the Greek language and customs predominated, as is clearly proven by the antiquities discovered in Herculaneum and Pompeii. After the third century, when the Romans conquered the peninsula, they held possession, and gradually introduced the'r language and civilization, and it is only in certain remote districts that traces of the Greek language and customs can now be discovered.

A long and earnestly cherished desire to visit Pompeii can now be gratified. We reach the exhumed city by railroad, a distance of fourteen miles, in fifty minutes. Paying the entrance fee of two francs, a guide is assigned us, who conducts us through the city and gives us a very intelligible explanation of the different points of interest, though his knowledge of the English language is rather limited. The approach to the principal gate is up a rather steep ascent, for the city is situated on a hill. We first visit a small museum near the entrance, where many exhumed relics are deposited, the most interesting of which are several bodies taken from the ruins, some of them recently. A complete impression of the bodies in the positions they occupied after they were overwhelmed was made in the ashes and scoriæ before the flesh could have disintegrated and dropped away, thus leaving only the bones. In some cases where these moulds were preserved in a sufficiently perfect state they were filled with plaster, and so the exact shape and attitude of the deceased at the moment they were overwhelmed has been preserved.

We pass on and enter one of the principal streets of the exhumed city. We visit a good many of the houses, but as they are constructed upon the same general plan a description of one is sufficient. The main difference consists in the size of the rooms and style of ornamentation. The entrance to the house leads directly into the atrium, an open court, with a fountain in the centre. Back of this is an apartment which we should call a reception-room, where the owner of the house received his friends and business acquaintances. Back of this room was an open court, surrounded by columns, which was the general family apartment. On each side of all these central apartments were the sleeping and eating rooms of the family, and other rooms for domestic uses.

The sleeping-rooms were generally very small. The paintings were all in fresco upon the walls, and in some of the buildings of the wealthy inhabitants they were very fine. The general tone of the artistic work, both of the statuary and paintings, is luxurious, and in many cases somewhat erotic, plainly indicating the ease-loving and pleasure-seeking character of the inhabitants. A large amount of wonderful statuary, and also various kinds of ornamental articles, have been removed and deposited in the museum at Naples as the excavations from time to time have brought them to light. In many cases the mural paintings have also been sawed off from the walls and deposited in the same place. The latter, however, is not allowed any more, and so the paintings which are now discovered remain in their original positions. The second story was appropriated to the slaves.

The fact that the principal public buildings have been already disclosed indicates that the central portion of the city has been opened up. Among these are the Forum, the Temple of Jupiter, Temple of Mercury, Temple of Venus, the Basilica, etc., etc., and the great theatre. The latter especially has been admirably preserved. The stage, the pit, the elevated seats back of the latter, and even the galleries are exactly as they were eighteen hundred years ago.

With a little aid of the imagination one can picture the scenes that transpired here in that far-off age, the social intercourse, the public displays, the legislation, the administration of justice, and indeed one can almost see the happy faces peering out of the carriages whose wheels have worn deep furrows in the large stone blocks with which the streets are paved. There can be no deception here, as in many of the so-called sacred places and relics that challenge the credulity of the traveller in the Holy Land. There are the veritable grooves in the solid stone blocks, in many cases cut so deep that it would seem not improbable that the wheels were rolling over them at the very moment when Christ was born in Bethlehem.

The little city is supposed to have contained some 20,000 inhabitants, and was no doubt a prosperous, thriving place, as there are many indications that it was the seat of considerable local traffic. There are several wine-shops containing the identical stone jars that the wine was drawn from to supply the customers of their former owners. These were of extraordinary size, some of them being of the capacity of two or three barrels each. But we must leave this most fascinating spot and return to the city, passing Herculaneum on our way, which lies more directly at the foot of Mount Vesuvius.

The second great point of interest here is the museum, a visit to which has delighted us more than we can describe. It is the great depository of the works of art and relics that have been exhumed from the buried cities of Herculaneum and Pompeii, and is devoted almost exclusively to them. The building is very magnificent and expensive, being entirely fire-proof, and the collection is most admirably arranged and grouped. It is said here to be one of the largest and richest collections of ancient statuary in the world.

As one wanders through the magnificent halls and feasts his eyes upon these rare masterpieces of art, which so unmistakably mark the distant era in which they were produced as the golden age of statuary, he may well realize that he is enjoying a treat which never in the course of his future life will be repeated, unless, fortunately, he may some time visit it again, after the collection shall have been enriched by additions from the same sources, the results of future excavations.

The appearance of the statues in the collection indicates unmistakably which of the two buried cities they were exhumed from. Those taken from Herculaneum are quite brown and discolored, that city having been overwhelmed by a stream of lava, which, of course, reached the city while it was yet hot; but Pompeii was covered deep with the ashes and scoriæ which were thrown from the crater, and probably drifted in that direction by the wind. The latter materials being lighter and not so hot, the statuary and other art treasures were not so much injured, and many of them are exhumed in a comparatively perfect state, after having laid in their tomb for eighteen hundred years.

The museum is specially rich in bronzes from the two cities, the extreme delicacy and beauty of which convey to us an idea of the height to which this art had been cultivated. The causes alluded to above have produced somewhat analogous effects upon the bronzes, those taken from Herculaneum being of a dark green hue, produced by the pressure of the great masses of hot lava, while those from Pompeii are of a light blue and green tinge, and somewhat oxidized from exposure to greater moisture.

Where there is such a wilderness of richness and beauty we can only generalize. The government certainly deserve great credit for the manner in which they have preserved and arranged this wonderful collection.

We have visited many other places which we have not the space to describe, the royal palaces, the aquarium, the catacombs, the tomb of Virgil, who wrote many of his beautiful works here, etc., etc., and we will close with a ride through the old part of the city. The streets here are mostly very narrow, many of them not more than six or eight feet wide, and the houses are very high. In many cases it would be easy for the neighbors to shake hands with each other across the street from the upper stories, for there is often less space between the houses in the upper than in the lower part of them.

The population is very dense and the sanitary arrangements exceedingly imperfect. The cholera two years ago swept away five hundred victims a day from this part of the city. We return to our hotel by a drive past the public gardens on the principal promenade of the city, bordering on the bay.

The Hotel de Vesuvius has been recently erected, and is entirely in the Pompeian style of architecture and decorations, and is certainly a most harmonious and beautiful building. It is one of the best and most honestly conducted hotels we have ever met with in any country, and is delightfully situated upon the bay directly opposite Mount Vesuvius.

We have witnessed the only eruption from the crater that we have seen during our visit as we rose from bed this morning, at a very early hour, to leave the city. But we must bid good-by to Naples and depart for Rome, the next goal on our homeward journey.

LETTER XIV.

A Sight of Vesuvius in Eruption—Leaving Naples and the Journey to Rome—In the Holy City—A Visit to St. Peter's Church—Its Marvels—The Vatican, the Pope's Prison—Galleries of Pictures and Statuary—The Capitol Museum—Other Attractions, etc., etc.

Rome, February 10, 1886.

HAVING risen early this morning to complete our arrangements for leaving Naples, we were favored with the sight of an eruption from Vesuvius, which had hitherto, during our visit here, been emitting great clouds of smoke only. It was just before the dawn of day, and as it was a dark morning the effect was grand.

Regretting the necessity of cutting short our visit to this famed spot, and taking one more view of the beautiful bay with its unrivalled environments, we enter the train and pass rapidly northwards. A short ride on an admirable stone ballasted railroad brings us to hoary old Rome. The scenery is beautiful. The railroad runs through a valley most of the distance, and hundreds of men and women are digging up the ground with spades, while in the whole distance we only saw one man using a plough for that purpose, which was drawn by a pair of feeble-looking oxen. Although we are in the midst of a civilization in which one would naturally look for the adoption of the modern appliances for cultivating the soil, which have so thoroughly revolutionized the old methods in our own country, we are surprised to find a prevalence of the old methods and the almost universal use of the old implements.

We become aware that the great city is not far distant by the sight of many curious things, the most striking of which is a stone aqueduct, stretching far out into the Campagna. It is built upon stone arches and stands high above the plain. In many places the structure seems to be complete for long distances, when suddenly a break occurs and a few arches are missing, the only indication, as we view it from the window of the car, that it is a ruin.

The scene at the station in Rome is almost a duplicate of that which is daily witnessed at the stations of all the principal cities of the United States. The principal hotels have their busses on hand to receive guests, and you are even addressed in English in many cases, as the porters usually manage enough of that language to use on such occasions, and they are very expert in detecting the nationality of the traveller by his general appearance. We soon find ourselves comfortably housed at the Hotel de Londres. The house is filled with guests, as the leading hotels in Rome always are at this season, just before the carnival opens.

There is every indication that the history of this wonderful city extends far back into the remote past. But the history of its origin must necessarily be largely a matter of conjecture. The story of Romulus and Remus fixes the date of the foundation of the city 753 B.C. But there can be no reasonable doubt that it is much older than this.

To visit St. Peter's Church at Rome has been the dream of our life, and now the fascinating dream is about to become a reality. We approach the noble edifice with reverent steps. It is not sacred to us, we must confess, because of the religious associations clustering around it, but because of its grand proportions, its sublime beauty, its inspiring harmony; because it was conceived and projected into being by the action of the divine influx of harmony upon the human faculties. Underlying the claims of the ecclesiastical body who dominate here, as to the sacredness of the building, and the infallibility of their system of faith and worship, there must, of necessity, be much that is unreliable, since it is the result of many centuries of crude experiences, and has crystallized into its present form through the gradual development of the religious faculties of a long succession of fallible men, many of them filled with narrow and crude ideas which they in turn had inherited. But no broad-minded man can stand in this presence and gaze at this noble structure, and take in its grand proportions, without realizing something of the inspiration through which it was conceived and the genius by which it was embodied.

The immediate approach to St. Peter's is exceedingly imposing. It consists of a grand plaza over ten hundred feet long by about six hundred feet wide. On the sides are two semi-circular colonnades, supported by nearly four hundred columns and buttresses, and crowned by one hundred and twenty-six statues of saints. In the centre of the plaza stands the great obelisk brought from Egypt some three hundred years ago, which is flanked by two beautiful fountains, constantly pouring forth copious streams of sparkling water. These stand opposite the centre of the colonnades, and altogether the effect is harmonious and beautiful.

All these things combined, the ample space, the tall, tapering obelisk, the graceful fountains, and the wonderful double colonnades, form a most appropriate approach to the largest and grandest church in the world.

The front is one hundred and forty-four feet in height, and is crowned with statues of Christ and the apostles nineteen feet high. From the grand entrance, which is three hundred and eighty feet long, we pass into the church itself. As we gaze up into the vast dome a feeling of awe pervades us, which is succeeded by a consciousness of personal insignificance.

We now make the ascent, which will enable us to view the vast structure from the different points of elevation. Reaching the base of the dome, we begin to realize the great size of the building, and the beauty and harmony of its proportions. A good illustration of the latter is furnished by the fact that the foot of a cherub in mosaic is as long as a man's arm from the elbow to the hand, though when viewed from the floor below the figure seems of natural size.

We ascend to the top of the dome, and even climb up into the ball, which we find large enough to contain a dozen men in standing position, though it looks from the street below only about the size of a man's head. A most superb view is here obtained of the city, the cathedral, and the surrounding country.

The main structure was built after the plans of Bramante. It was not finished during his lifetime, and Michael Angelo, who succeeded him in charge of the work, completed the edifice according to the original plans. The dome was the work of Michael Angelo, and was finished strictly according to his plans, though it was not completed until after his death.

We return to St. Peter's repeatedly during the brief visit we are enabled to make here, and every time with increased enjoyment of its beauty and grandeur.

Passing to the left on leaving the church we enter the Vatican, the residence of the pope—or rather his prison, as he terms it, for he never goes outside the grounds since he has been deprived of the civil power. Indeed, it is more than whispered that he does not dare to pass the limits of the Vatican, so strong is the feeling of the Jesuits, on account of the divorcement of the civil from the religious functions of the pope. But the people of Italy have a voice in this matter, and from present indications the pope will not only die in the harness in his prison, but his successor will enter *his* prison for life when he assumes the functions of his office.

The point of absorbing interest in the Vatican is the fact that it is the receptacle of so many rare and valuable works of art, and we hasten to get such a view of them as the time at our disposal may allow. The picture-galleries are mostly at the very top of the different buildings comprising the Vatican, where the best light can be obtained. The wealth of art stored here is almost inconceivable to one who has not visited these galleries, and one is dazed on finding himself face to face with such a number of works of the old masters, about the authenticity of which there cannot be the least doubt, and feels how feeble is the attempt at particular description, when a single gem of Titian, or Raphael, or Domenichino can only begin to be appreciated after hours and hours of patient study. Passing through gallery after gallery filled to repletion with the best productions of a host of the most celebrated artists of the past, we descend to the street again, feeling that life is not long enough to properly see all that there is to see of art in this grand old city of Rome.

The gallery of statuary is reached by a detour round St. Peter's, quite a long walk, affording an excellent view of the exterior of the church on all sides and a good idea of its immense proportions. The same remarks apply to the statuary as to the paintings. A single statue possesses in itself a value beyond all money estimate. The Romans regard the Apollo Belvedere with the same reverence and guard it with the same watchfulness and zealous care as the Parisians do their Venus de Milo. It has no money value, and could not be bought. This statue possesses a most singular and fascinating beauty, and produces rather the idea of grace and dignity than of massiveness and strength.

We visit the Capitol Museum especially to see the Dying Gladiator. It was found in the gardens of Sallust with other statues, and is a most wonderful work. The right arm was restored by Michael Angelo, and is an excellent specimen of his great skill. The domain of art is so extensive here, and it is so utterly impossible for any one, and especially one whose knowledge of art is limited, to do anything like justice to it, that we despair of saying much that can interest the reader. We certainly are deriving great satisfaction from even a cursory view of the celebrated works that are scattered in great profusion through the numerous galleries that are accessible to the public. Besides the strictly public galleries many of the old palaces have galleries attached to them filled with choice works, and they are open to the public on certain specified days, and on those days they are thronged with visitors.

But there are many other points of interest in Rome which may perhaps prove equally noteworthy, some of which we propose to describe in our next letter.

LETTER XV.

Yet Tarrying in Rome—More of the Sights of the Ancient City—Italy and America Wedded—Increase of Art Taste—The Colosseum—The Forum—Other Celebrated Structures—The Pantheon—The King's Residence—Castle of St. Angelo—Ruins of the Baths of Caracalla—The Catacombs, etc., etc.

ROME, February 15, 1886.

BUT for the apprehension that our readers may think we have failed to give them such a description as might be warranted by the opportunities enjoyed here, we should mention the fact that we are especially fortunate in having an introduction to the private secretary to the king of Italy, S. Sirovich, Esq., who is an Italian and has lived in Rome all his life. Through him we gain access to many places we could not otherwise see. Not the least interesting of these is his own house, where we are most cordially welcomed and hospitably entertained.

Italy and America are wedded in this household, Mr. Sirovich having married the daughter of one of our most celebrated artists, who has spent the greater part of his life in Rome. She has lost none of her affection for America, and not only takes us to her heart and home, but constitutes herself our guide, and goes with us everywhere, and, of course, gives us many interesting particulars that we should otherwise fail to acquire.

We find in the studio of an English artist who has spent his life in Rome an item of especial interest. Some two years since he received an order from Mrs. Mitchell, wife of Alex. Mitchell, the great railroad millionaire of the northwest, who resides at Milwaukee, for a pair of colossal St. Bernard dogs, and they are now completed and ready for shipment. This artist has a special talent for reproducing animals in marble, and has certainly achieved a notable result in these two dogs. They are made of the purest white Carrara marble, and are exceedingly life like and beautiful. It is to be hoped that Mrs. Mitchell will give her countrymen an opportunity to see these gems of art before they are placed in her own home.

It is certainly a most gratifying fact that our countrywoman, who has such ample means at her command, is disposed to use it for the encouragement of art. That a better day for art is dawning upon us in the western world is plainly indicated by the fact that so many of our wealthy countrymen are using their means in the most effective way to promote its advancement. In the intense scramble for money-making men are very apt to come to think that there is no higher aim in life than the piling up of riches, and any indication of a better state of mind in this regard is certainly gratifying. Many a struggling artist in Rome and other art centres of Europe has reaped the benefit of this growing sentiment in the orders that he has received from the class alluded to. Americans spend their money with proverbial freedom, and of late years they have been less disposed to waste it on comparatively worthless objects, and more inclined to invest in works of art that have a permanent value.

Next to St. Peter's in point of interest is the Colosseum. This was the largest theatre building in the world, being capable of holding almost one hundred thousand people. Although large quantities of the material have been removed for building purposes, about one-third of the structure remains. In one portion it stands to the height of four very high stories, and this is the best preserved part of the ruin. Some portions of the seats and their foundations are well preserved. In the lower part of the structure, beneath the amphitheatre, were dens for the wild beasts used in the gladiatorial displays, and during an early period they had an apparatus by means of which the arena was flooded, and naval contests formed part of the amusements of the people.

Near the Colosseum is the Roman Forum, also one of the most remarkable ruins of the city. It occupies an immense space and embraces within its area several important ruins, the Temple of Saturn, the Column of Phocas, the Temple of Castor, etc. The Forum was the great popular place for the gatherings of the Roman people, and was situated in the very midst of old Rome. Beyond the Forum and also near the Colosseum is the immense Arch of Constantine, from the summit of which a most magnificent panoramic view of Rome is obtained. Also the Arch of Titus, another old landmark, stands near. On the west side of the Forum rises the Palatine Hill, containing some of the oldest and most remarkable ruins in the city.

The Palace of the Cæsars is here, the dwelling of Cicero, and the house of Nero. We entered the sleeping-room of the latter and his dining-room, both of which have well-preserved frescos upon their walls. The Palace of Caligula is also within the enclosure, with its immense, gloomy dungeons beneath.

The Pantheon, formerly a heathen temple, now a church, is said to be the only building of ancient Rome that has been preserved in its entirety. It is lighted by a large aperture at the top of the dome. This is never closed, and the effect is peculiar. At present there is an immense number of wreaths on the floor and at the entrance and on the pavement in front, placed there in honor of Victor Emmanuel.

We visit the Quirinal Palace, the residence of King Humbert and his beautiful wife. It is situated on one of the three parallel hills of the Quirinal. The king and queen are very popular, and are much beloved by their subjects. We are fortunate enough to meet them in the street returning from a ride. They are readily distinguished by the red livery of their escort, no one else being allowed to use that color.

The Castle of St. Angelo is an exceedingly interesting old pile. It is circular in form, and stands near the end of the bridge we cross to go to St. Peter's. It is distinguished as having been the prison of Beatrice Cenci. It is now used as a military prison. A magnificent view of St. Peter's is obtained from its summit, and the grand dome looks larger and more imposing from this point than from the street nearer to the church itself.

We should be glad to try to say something interesting of very many places visited within the city limits—the churches, the monuments, the fountains, promenades, street scenes, shops, theatres, villas, and public and private buildings—but there is a limit to the time and space properly appropriated to such a purpose, and we will therefore visit some of the interesting scenes and localities outside the walls.

Passing out in the direction of the Appian way, immediately to the right, and not far from the gate by which we leave the city, are the ruins of the baths of Caracalla. They were capable of accommodating sixteen hundred bathers at once. All the statues and works of art were long ago removed and placed in the different museums in Rome, and there is now little left except the massive walls and here and there a bit of the tessellated pavement. The place is so immense, the walls so massive and grand, that it is difficult to realize that it was ever used as a bath, it is so unlike any existing place for the same purpose. The effect of the Cyclopean walls towering high above our heads, as we walk through the deserted and dismantled courts below, is exceedingly weird and spectre-like.

The Catacombs of Calixtus next claim our

attention. Beyond these, and situated at greater or less distances from the main road, are several groups of catacombs, which are much frequented by visitors, and are full of interest to such of them as have archæological tastes.

We reach the Appian way proper, and discover here and there bits of the original solid stone pavement, which consists of large square blocks of granite, that appear to be cemented in their places, seem to have stood the wear and tear of centuries, and to be capable of a repetition of the same for other future centuries. Further out, the Appian way is flanked with a succession of ancient tombs, most of them in a dismantled condition, the statues and other artistic ornaments having been removed and placed in the public museums of Rome. Pausing at this point we refresh ourselves with a bottle of excellent wine, costing only half a franc (ten cents), and return to the city just in season to escape the unhealthy evening air of the Campagna.

By a ride of about two miles from the same gate in another direction we reach the Church of St. Paul, which very few visitors to Rome fail to see. One naturally wonders why such a magnificent church should be erected two miles from the city, but an explanation is furnished by the knowledge of the fact that in the palmy days of Rome the city extended so far out upon the Campagna as to bring this church quite within its limits.

It is interesting to observe the striking contrast in the architecture of the new parts of Rome and the specimens that are still extant here which were produced by Bramante and Michael Angelo and other great architects of their time. The period in which they lived and embodied their conceptions seems to have witnessed the high-water mark of excellence in this line. Indeed, the same is true of painting and sculpture. Though mighty struggles have been made since in this direction, the old standard of excellence has never been reached in either of these departments of art.

LETTER XVI.

Leaving Rome—A Country of many Railroad Tunnels—The Carrara Marble Quarries—Pisa and its Leaning Tower and other Attractions—Genoa, the Principal Seaport of Italy—Milan—"The Last Supper"—The Great Cathedral—Description thereof—View from its Tower—Leaving Milan—The Alps Scenery—Arrival at Basle.

BASLE, February 20, 1886.

LEAVING Rome and entering upon a most picturesque route by railroad, we pass rapidly northward, with the Mediterranean on the left and the beautiful Apennine mountains on the right. An extraordinary feature of this route is the large number of promontories that project into the Mediterranean, which are penetrated by tunnels for the passage of the railroad. There are thirty tunnels between Pisa and Genoa alone.

Avensa is a small town on the road from Pisa and Genoa, and possesses a harbor, which is used mainly for shipping marble from the celebrated quarries of Carrara, which are reached by a short digression to the right over a branch railroad. There are some hundreds of these quarries, employing thousands of workmen, and most of the statuary marble, as well as large quantities used for building purposes, comes from these quarries, and much is exported to France, England, America, and other countries.

Returning to the main road and proceeding northwards, we soon reach Pisa, as a passing glimpse of the celebrated leaning tower informs us. This is perhaps the first object of interest to the traveller, and a very remarkable one it certainly is. Pisa is said to have produced more celebrated architects than any other city in Italy, and it possesses itself several remarkable specimens of their skill. The leaning tower has eight different stories, and is built twelve feet out of perpendicular; but whether this was by accident or design it is now quite impossible to tell. This structure, together with the Piazza del Duomo, the cathedral, the baptistry, and the cemetery, comprise a most extraordinary group, the inspection of which completes a day of unusual interest, and involves an experience that the traveller would be loath to omit.

We now reach Genoa, and the first thought that occurs to an American on entering the city naturally is that it is the birth-place of Christopher Columbus. Genoa is the principal seaport of Italy, and possesses a beautiful harbor and substantial piers. The exports are mostly the fruits of the country, and its imports from Great Britain, the United States, and other countries largely exceed the exports. Its situation is one of extreme beauty, the streets being terraced one above another upon the abrupt hillside. The city is very old, and is replete with historic buildings and works of art, in the examination of which the tourist can most pleasantly and profitably spend a few days.

At this point we leave the coast of the Mediterranean and travel toward the interior of northern Italy, and soon reach Milan, a large and wealthy manufacturing city, situated in the centre of the Lombardy district. The principal manufactures are of silk, rich tapestries, and kid gloves One firm of glove-makers, which employs three hundred hands, sell their entire product to a single New York house.

The two leading considerations which inspired our visit to this city were the view of "The Last Supper," the great masterpiece of Leonardo da Vinci, and the great cathedral. Our first visit is to the church containing the painting. We find it upon the end wall of a long, narrow chapel, which is said to have formerly been used as the dining-room of the monks. The room is cold and the surroundings uninviting. The great work is in fresco, and is in a dilapidated condition. The surface seems blistered, and in many places small patches have peeled off; but the outline and the wonderful expression of the faces are still well preserved, and, as it is evident that no attempt at restoration is allowed, we may reasonably hope that for many generations it may remain and constitute, as it does now, an object of veneration and an inexpressible source of delight to thousands and thousands of future worshippers at the shrine of the great master.

The Cathedral of Milan is regarded by the Milanese with especial veneration and affection. It is the third church in size in Europe, St. Peter's and the cathedral at Seville being the only larger ones. The plan is said to have been copied after that of the great cathedral at Cologne, which was commenced several hundred years earlier, and was altogether eleven hundred years in process of erection, and has been but recently completed and dedicated. It is one of the finest specimens of pure Gothic architecture in Europe.

It is almost five hundred feet long by one hundred and eighty-six feet wide. There are fifty-two immense pillars supporting the interior, each fifteen feet in diameter. These are adorned with niches containing marble statues instead of capitals, producing a very odd and peculiar effect. The distinguishing characteristic of the building is the immense number of marble statues with which it is adorned in all parts, inside and outside. There are already forty-five hundred of these, and there are many niches yet to be filled. There are one hundred Gothic turrets on the roof, and others are being added from year to year, and each one is capped with a marble statue. Every statue in the building is of solid marble, and is made with reference to the special position it occupies. The result is a grand and harmonious structure.

We ascend to the highest accessible point in the tower, and the view obtained amply compensates us for the labor. The beautiful city lies at our feet, and almost all of northern Italy is within the range of vision. Beyond the border Mont Cenis, and still farther in the distance grand old Mont Blanc tower up against the distant horizon, and further to the right the Bernese Alps, the summits of the St. Gothard, and other high peaks complete a scene of great beauty and grandeur.

Conspicuous among the many other great churches here worthy of a visit is the Church of St. Ambrosio, in the architecture and decorations of which three distinct civilizations are plainly indicated: first, the heathen (who used it as a temple of Bacchus); second, the pagan; and third, the first Catholic. There are here rude pillars and other fragments taken from the old Temple of Bacchus, which are more than two thousand years old.

In a drive through the city and suburbs we pass the Arc de Triomphe, which stands opposite the military plaza. The latter is one of the finest squares in Europe for military displays, comprising three hundred acres in the heart of the city. One side of it is occupied with extensive barracks.

We leave Milan in the early morning, so as to enjoy a daylight view of the scenery of the Alps. We soon pass the frontier, catching a glimpse of the beautiful Lake Como; and now begins the ascent, which soon brings us to the region of snow. We pass through twenty-four small tunnels on the Italian side and eighteen on the Swiss side, besides the main tunnel, which is nine and three-quarter miles long, and requires twenty minutes to pass through.

The crossing of the St. Gothard by means of these tunnels is a wonderful piece of engineering. At one point on the Italian side the tunnel was excavated into the mountain in a spiral form on an up-grade, making the circuit by blasting through solid rock, and so coming out again almost directly over the point of entrance, the up-grade in making the circuit giving the elevation. This process is repeated three times, and after the third circuit is completed the railroad and the mouths of the tunnels where the train entered the mountain are distinctly visible at three points below, one above the other, and a small village in the valley below comes in sight three times, and at the completion of each circuit it looks more distant as a higher elevation is attained.

The above is well illustrated by penetrating a cork with a corkscrew and cutting it in the middle vertically. The road is splendidly built, and the trains are run with the utmost care, and no serious accident has occurred on this line since it was opened. This route is more interesting, and affords a more picturesque view of the Alps, than that by Mont Cenis tunnel.

Descending into Switzerland, we soon leave the region of snow, and in time reach Basle, where a good supper awaits us, and a comfortable compartment on the train for our long night-ride to Paris.

LETTER XVII.

Palestine and Paris Contrasted—First Impression of the Latter City—An Art Loving People—Moving the Statue of the Venus de Milo—A Contrast in Steps—The Hotels of Paris—The Restaurants—Wine Consumption—The French Great Lovers of Amusement—Grand Opera House—The Art-Galleries and their Treasures—Various Points of Interest.

PARIS, February 25, 1886.

PALESTINE and Paris. Type of the old; symbol of the new. One the embodiment of the ideas and spirit of the oldest civilization; the other the very home of modern æsthetic culture. One the storehouse of the methods adopted and results obtained two thousand years ago; the other the receptacle of the rich fruits of the civilization of the nineteenth century. One inhabited by a people who live in tents as their fathers did, or in dwellings in the construction of which no innovation has been made in the lapse of twenty centuries; the other luxuriating in homes that have not only required in their constructio he utmost skill of cunning architects, the highest talent of a succession of skilful artists, and the combined efforts of a host of workmen, each gifted in his own specialty, but laying under contribution for its proper furnishing every country, civilized and uncivilized, in the four quarters of the globe. The sudden passing from one of these extreme civilizations to the other serves to make a vivid impression upon the mind and materially to heighten the contrast.

The earlier letters of this series have embodied the record of the impressions produced by our visit to Palestine. We have now to do with Paris, of which so much may be said that we are embarrassed to say fittingly the little we have to say.

The first impression made upon the mind of the visitor here is that produced by the prevalence of the sense of harmony and beauty that all classes seem to possess. The contrast in this regard with other nations is most marked. In Eastern countries not only are the higher considerations of art neglected, but all sanitary considerations are ignored; the sewage is allowed to lie in the gutters on the surface of the streets, the manure is piled up in great heaps to lie festering in the sun, filling the air with pestilential odors, while there appears to be an utter unconsciousness on the part of the people that anything is amiss.

The contrast in this regard between Paris and the other great cities in civilized countries, while it may not be as sweeping, is yet very marked. This fine artistic taste and sense of harmony and beauty seems everywhere present in Paris. While it shows itself in a marked degree in the great art-galleries, it is plainly recognized in every department of construction. It is especially noticeable in the construction of the clothing of all classes, even of the servants. The washerwomen and the chambermaids have perfect fitting waists. It seems as difficult to get a badly fitting garment here as it is elsewhere to procure a perfect fitting one. This fine artistic taste is nowhere more noticeable than in the architecture.

Everything in Paris is pleasing and satisfying, while in London, for instance, a nice sense of proportion and acute perception of beauty and harmony is violated by structures which meet the eye on every hand. The same is true of the carriages and furniture. John Bull is proverbially solid and substantial, and his carriages and his furniture, and all his belongings, are like him—solid, heavy. But the element of beauty and gracefulness which the facile Frenchman, and the American, too, for that matter, would manage to combine with the substantial, is often lacking in the Englishman's result. This is true even of the cooking utensils. Those of the Englishman are tremendously solid and useful, but quite devoid of graceful curves or artistic effects, while the same articles in the Frenchman's kitchen are so graceful and elegant that the very sight of them inspires one with an appetite.

There is some objection to the uniformity in the style of the buildings in the business blocks in Paris, but at the same time there is great advantage in it, as it serves to prevent the incongruous results that would arise from following the plans prescribed by the architects, or the more crude fancies of the owners. The general excellence of the designs from which the public as well as the private buildings are constructed, and the great attention given to art in every department, has reacted with most beneficial effect upon the common people. Indeed, very many of the latter are no mean judges of art. When a new public building is inaugurated, or work of art opened for exhibition, the people are present in great numbers, and their comments are often as judicious and appreciative as those of persons who possess more knowledge in such matters.

Any notable art event attracts universal attention. Not long since the famous statue, the Venus de Milo, was moved from the position it had long occupied in the Louvre into another room and placed in a new light. The event stirred the whole of Paris. All classes came to see it in the new position and to criticise the change. Parisians of every degree, high and low, almost worship this statue, which, mutilated as it is, is perhaps the most beautiful statue in the world. A proposition to purchase it for its weight in gold would be instantly and indignantly refused. The attempt to move this statue from Paris would create a revolution.

It is wonderful how little there is to offend the eye as one examines the buildings, monuments, and works of art here. Every flight of steps, indeed, every individual step, is in itself a work of art, "a thing of beauty." To go up such a flight of stairs as may be met anywhere in Paris is no hardship, while to go down them is a positive luxury. In striking contrast with these is a flight of five steps at the New York terminus of our great Brooklyn bridge. I never go up or down those five narrow, abrupt steps without getting angry, and any Parisian architect who could be guilty of producing such a flight of steps would hang himself from sheer mortification.

There might be some excuse for such a result if the space was limited, but one can see no reason why the ascent should not be made by five or six wide, graceful steps instead of by the narrow, steep ones now in use; and it would be a most encouraging sign if the people of New York would demand the change of the bridge authorities, with such vehemence and persistence that they would be compelled to concede it. The great bridge itself is a work of such wonderful beauty that it seems like the creation of a master, while some bungler has been entrusted with the construction of those five steps.

But we must not forget that we are in Paris, not in New York. It is said that Parisians have no home life; and the fact that they spend so much of their time in the restaurants and cafés would seem to indicate that there is some basis for the imputation. It is almost a necessity, however, with them to spend an hour or two after lunch and dinner at their favorite café, with their cigarette and coffee. Various grades of light amusements are furnished at many of the cafés. The restaurants are also a peculiar feature of Paris, and they are well patronized— so many, both residents and strangers, live in lodgings and take their meals at the most convenient restaurants.

The hotels are numerous and afford a wide range of choice. If one wishes to be near the centre of fashion he will choose a hotel in the vicinity of the Grand Opera House, where most of the first-class and expensive houses are situated. There are many good houses in less central locations, which afford excellent accommodations at much less prices. We find such a house in the Hôtel Britannique, Avenue Victoria. It is situated in a good location near Rue Rivoli, and not far from the Louvre, and is a clean, well kept, and comfortable house, with excellent table and moderate charges.

Wine is the universal accompaniment of all meals in Paris, the coffee and roll taken on rising being hardly considered a meal. Good claret may be obtained at a good price, but there is an immense amount of poor stuff consumed. It is computed that one hundred million gallons of wine are consumed annually in Paris. France is the home of the vine, and even now, though her vineyards have been terribly devastated by the phylloxera for a series of years, she still produces some eight hundred million gallons of wine annually, most of which is consumed at home. There can be no reasonable doubt that the destruction of the vineyards of France would be a national calamity, as the substitution of distilled liquors for the wines now consumed would tend to convert them from a nation of temperate people into a nation of drunkards.

The French are proverbially an amusement-loving people, and the numerous theatres of Paris are all well patronized. The Grand Opera House is the most sumptuous theatre in the world, and probably the most costly. It occupies one of the most central and prominent squares in the city, and a large number of old buildings were demolished to make room for it. Indeed, many hundred buildings in the vicinity were swept away, and the streets and avenues reconstructed and studded with new buildings, made to harmonize with the architecture of the Opera House and give it a proper setting.

A good illustration of the attention given to artistic effects in Paris is furnished by the fact that the principal avenue leading from the front of the Opera House was constructed without the trees that the original plan embraced, because they would obstruct the view and hide the grand proportions of the building as it is approached by this avenue.

Prominent among the points of interest for the visitor in Paris are the art-galleries. Those which are accessible to the public are so numerous and extensive that no satisfactory examination can be made of their contents in any limited space of time. As in Rome even one who possesses culture and knowledge in matters of art must spend a lifetime in order to begin to comprehend its treasures, so in Paris one without such special culture and knowledge is still more at a loss to comprehend the great works that meet his gaze on every hand, much less to write intelligently about them. It is said that there is a larger number of private collections of valuable works of art in Paris than in any other city in the world.

There are so many points of interest here that one is at a loss to know where to begin, especially as the brief space of a single letter affords so little opportunities for extended description or comment.

The streets, boulevards, and public squares are admirably planned and constructed, and with many of them are associated numerous historical incidents of great interest and importance.

The Place de la Concorde is the most extensive and beautiful of the promenades in Paris, and is ripe in historical associations. It was here that the guillotine commenced its bloody work, claiming among its first victims Louis XVI., Charlotte Corday, and Marie Antoinette. During the Reign of Terror thus inaugurated some three thousand lives were sacrificed in the space of about two years.

The Place de la Concorde and the Champs Elysées form one grand avenue several hundred feet wide, studded with several rows of trees, and flanked with splendid residences, and most appropriately terminating with the Arc de Triomphe, constituting one of the most charming promenades in the world. The Triumphal Arch is the grandest structure of this description in the world, and the view of Paris and vicinity from its summit is very fine.

From this point a series of grand avenues radiate to different parts of Paris. We will take the one leading to the Bois de Boulogne. This was formerly a grand hunting-ground, and was frequented by duelists and bandits, but is now a large and magnificent park supported by the city.

Among the points of interest visited in and around this charming city we note the following as especially worthy of attention:

The Invalides, an institution established by the government as a home for disabled soldiers. The buildings are very extensive, but the main point of attraction is the grand gilded dome, a conspicuous object from every part of Paris, under which is the sepulchre of Napoleon I., a simple but most artistic and impressive monument, and cherished by the French people with great veneration.

The Louvre, with its interminable galleries filled with priceless treasures of art.

The Palais Royal, built early in the seventeenth century by Cardinal Richelieu as a residence for himself.

The Tuileries, one of the largest and grandest royal residences ever constructed, devastated by an armed mob during the French Revolution, and again by the Communists in 1871.

The Bastille, in whose dreary dungeons so many sons of France have languished in hopeless confinement.

Père La Chaise, the favorite burial-place of the Parisian.

Jardin des Plantes, with its extensive zoological museum, its valuable library of books and MSS. on natural history, and its unrivalled botanical collection.

The Gobelins, the government manufactory of the celebrated Gobelins tapestry, where many completed pieces of the production of these looms may be seen, as well as the actual process of producing them; one of the most interesting places in Paris.

The Pantheon, originally a temple devoted to the heroes and patriots of France, many of whom are buried within its walls, but now most inappropriately used as a church.

Notre Dame, one of the finest Gothic churches in Europe.

The Madeleine, a most imposing church building surrounded by massive columns, said to have been modelled after a Grecian temple, and at one time dedicated by Napoleon as a temple of glory.

The Catacombs, excavated during the Roman period to procure building stone, afterwards used as a receptacle for the dead.

St. Cloud, in the environs of the city, the favorite summer residence of Napoleon III.

Fontainebleau, with its old palace, so rich with historical associations, occupied successively by Henry IV., Louis XV., and Napoleon I.

St. Denis, where so many of the old monarchs of France are entombed.

Montmorency, noted for its having been one of the residences of Rousseau.

Sevres, celebrated for its government manufactory of fine porcelain.

Versailles, with its unrivalled fountains, famous palaces, with miles and miles of galleries filled with a bewildering mass of paintings and statuary.

Realizing how much that would prove interesting might be said by one visiting Paris with his eyes and ears open, with plenty of time at his disposal, and regretting that we have been able to say so little in the space of a single letter, we take leave of the gay capital.

LETTER XVIII.

Paris to London—Poor Railway Accommodations—Old London—Devastated by Fires, Pestilences, and Civil Wars—The Original City One Square Mile—Fragments of the Old Wall still Standing—Official Integrity—No Broadway Railroad Steal Possible here—Adhering to Old Methods—National Conceit—Antiquated Railroad Methods—Expressage Peculiarities—Underground, Surface, and Elevated or Upper Level Railroads—Ancient Guilds—Home Rule for Ireland—A London Banquet.

LONDON, February 28, 1886.

IT would be difficult to find a journey of the same length which is more dreaded by travellers than that between the two great capitals, Paris and London, where more discomforts are encountered and less accommodations are afforded than on any route of the same length in any country in the world which claims to furnish travellers the best railroad and steamboat facilities. On leaving Paris, although bearing first-class tickets, we are shut up in pens—called compartments—which are devoid of all those conveniences that the most ordinary cars have everywhere in America; and, after running the gauntlet of the terrible Channel, we find a duplicate of the French train we left an hour before awaiting us on the English side of the Channel, by which we complete the journey.

As we approach and enter the great city there can be no question as to its identity. It is unmistakably London. We are reminded of the description a young American woman once gave of the city, as she passed through on the elevated railroad, that "London consists chiefly of fog and smoke and chimney-pots." Coming, as we have, from the almost tropical climate of Palestine and Egypt, it seems especially cold and damp and forbidding here. But this is the season of the chilly east winds, and, no doubt, a change for the better may soon be looked for.

London has a well-defined history, extending over a period of several centuries. Back of the Roman invasion and settlement it was a mere village, a group of huts, but early in the Christian era it began to crystallize into a settlement of some importance, and at a very early period to show tokens of its future greatness. Some of the leading points of old London have a history reaching back to the ninth century, such as the Tower, St. Paul's Cathedral, and Westminster Abbey.

During the early history of the city, for several centuries, its slow but sure growth was often interrupted by devastating fires, pestilences, and civil wars. The terrible plague of 1664, which swept away one hundred thousand of the inhabitants, followed in 1666 by the great fire, which consumed some thirteen thousand dwellings, almost swept the city out of existence. But during the eighteenth century it recovered completely from these disasters and entered upon its wonderful career of future greatness.

The original city was comprised within the limits of one square mile, and its boundaries are still indicated here and there by fragments of the old wall which encompassed it. At the beginning of the eighteenth century the population was considerably less than one million. Now the square mile has expanded into more than two hundred and the population has swollen to the enormous aggregate of five millions, constituting it, beyond question, the largest city in the world.

Since the opening of the present century many important improvements and public works have been projected and completed under the superintendence of a body known as the Metropolitan Board of Works. The drainage of the city formerly passed into the Thames, which runs directly through it, and which thus became so polluted as to seriously endanger the public health. Since 1850 the Board have completed, at an enormous expense to the city, a system of sewerage connected with immense tunnels laid parallel with the Thames, which carries the sewage fourteen miles below the city, and pours it into the river at that point. But the city has extended with such rapid strides that this point is now within its limits and the old difficulty recurs again, and the water of the river is still polluted to an extent which endangers the health of the citizens.

An ingenious and novel plan has been perfected by Mr. J. M. Hart, a member of the present city council, for remedying the evil, and contracts are about to be given out to carry it into execution. The plan involves the construction of several immense pontoon-boats, which shall receive the entire contents of the sewers of the city, transport it out to sea, and deposit it beyond a point where its presence can in any way endanger the public health.

The manner in which the citizens sustain the authorities in matters of public moment is most admirable, and the interest they take in the progress of improvements for the benefit of the city has the effect of insuring faithful work and honesty of administration. Such an episode as the Broadway Railroad steal could hardly occur in London. Citizens accept office here and fill important public positions for the honor attached to such service, not for the purpose of "feathering their own nest," as is too often the case in America. The members of Parliament draw no salary, and there is no opportunity of "making money" out of the position. It would not do to say that there are no dishonest men in London, but it is quite evident that the standard of integrity is higher among officials here, and especially among those connected with the municipal government, than in our own country.

It is beautiful to gain a standpoint from which one can observe the excellencies or the faults of his own or another country without prejudice in favor of the one or against the other, and it is a sign of healthy growth when a people can bear to have the truth told them in regard to their shortcomings, and, at the same time, not "fall from grace" and lose their serenity of temper. The American people were very restive under the adverse criticisms recorded of them in the "American Notes," by Dickens, the result of his visit to our country some quarter of a century ago; but it is to be hoped, at least, that they have so far outgrown their childish sensitiveness that they could now receive a like rebuke for their foibles with sweetness and serenity, even though couched in language somewhat exaggerated and severe, and we feel entirely sure that John Bull will not wince in the least at any adverse criticisms we may be moved to make of his peculiarities or methods.

While there is much that is admirable and worthy of imitation here, there are many points in which the Englishman is behind his more enterprising neighbors on the other side of the Atlantic. One of the most marked characteristics of the Englishman is the tenacity with which he adheres to old methods, and his disinclination to change even when it is quite evident to everybody else, and one is tempted to think to himself too, that he is quite behind the age, and that the adoption of the new methods would prove a great saving of time and labor.

The characteristic Englishman cannot see that everything English is not the best. A given appliance or method has been used for a hundred years and answered the purpose, therefore it must be used for the next hundred, and no innovation, claiming to be an improvement, can replace it. Indeed, he will not admit that any valuable invention has ever been made outside of his own country, and especially in a new country like the United States. He will tell you gravely that the original idea of every improvement or innovation made in our country came from the Old World, and generally from England.

The national conceit of the Englishman of this class is something inconceivable. Indeed, this peculiarly strong innate sense of his own superiority is so marked that he can readily be distinguished from his fellow travellers in any part of the world by his bearing, and especially by his speech.

A good illustration of the peculiar methods which obtain here, in contrast with those in vogue in our own and other countries, is furnished by the construction, equipment, and management of the railroads. This contrast is most striking in the construction of the cars, the management of the baggage of passengers, and the manner in which the express business is done on the different roads. The cars are all of one pattern, the most luxurious and the most common. They are all constructed in compartments, each compartment accommodating eight people, facing each other, like an old-fashioned stage-coach. There are several such compartments on each set of trucks, the entrance being on the side, and there is no communication with any other part of the train.

There is a total absence of those toilet arrangements which conduce so much to the comfort and convenience of the traveller. Of course the passenger cannot have his baggage checked, and he must observe where it is placed, and he travels under constant apprehension of its loss; and if it is lost he is comforted with the assurance of the railroad officials that they will find it for him if they can. He is unable to produce the little brass check and demand the baggage or its equivalent. Doubtless it will take our dear old John Bull railroad director another score or two of years to see that by the check system *he* would be protected as well as the traveller, as he could then never deliver the baggage to the wrong person. He acknowledges that he is now very much annoyed by such wrong delivery, but has never devised any remedy, and, with the best remedy at hand in the American check-system, he shuts his eyes and plods along in the old ways.

Another peculiarity here is the manner in

which the express business is done. Each road has its own "parcels department," which does a business on its own line quite like that done by our express companies in America. Mr. Hart, the passenger agent of the Great Western Railway, to whom I had an introduction, politely explained to me the working of the parcels department of that mammoth corporation. Although it comes under Mr. Hart's supervision as passenger agent, this department is apparently as completely organized in every detail as our own great express companies, and the charges are more moderate than with us. They have an insurance department attached, so that one can insure the goods transmitted at the same time they are deposited with the company. I am indebted to Mr. Hart for much information in regard to the workings of this road. He is a very polite and cosmopolitan gentleman, and is much more liberal and progressive than the board of directors by whom he is controlled.

The network of railroads within the city limits, consisting of underground, surface, and elevated roads, is very extensive and complete. The latter are here called "upper level" roads. Between the bad air in the close compartments and the gas from the engines, travelling by these roads is very disagreeable and unhealthy; but hundreds of thousands are compelled to spend the best part of an hour every day in this vitiated atmosphere, greatly to their discomfort.

A marked feature here is the guilds, or city companies, of which there are about eighty in all, most of them very ancient, and several very wealthy, possessing vast estates. Some of them own immense properties in Ireland, and just at this moment there is a move to sell these Irish estates to the tenants, who have occupied them for many years. By the terms proposed ample time is given the purchasers, and every opportunity is afforded for them to become possessors of the soil; and it would seem that the successful adoption of the plan would form the best solution of the vexed problem of home rule in Ireland.

Some of these companies are very wealthy and influential, as the mercers, the fishmongers, the grocers, the ironmongers, the vintners, etc.; while others have no possessions, not even a hall in which to hold their annual meetings. My host here, being a member of one of these, has secured for me a ticket to their annual banquet. It is called the Fan-Makers Company. The Mercers Company most hospitably tendered them the use of their magnificent hall for the banquet. The members of the company, including a few invited guests, occupy the two hundred seats at the tables, every seat having been previously assigned to the occupant, and his name placed on the plate. The dinner is one of the kind in which the Englishman delights—"a big feed," as he designates it. It is a very dignified and formal affair. Every toast is "cut and dried," and some special individual is designated to respond to each in a speech which is evidently "cut and dried" also. Hence there is very little of that spontaneity which is the life of such an occasion, and I am not sorry to leave with my friend before the feast is concluded, to seek one more night's rest previous to encountering the perils of the last stage of our homeward journey.

LETTER XIX.

Leaving London for New York—Homeward Bound on the Ill-fated *Oregon*—A Faithful, Accurate, and Graphic Description of the Fearful Disaster—Behavior of the Officers and Crew—Heroism of the Passengers—On the Verge of Eternity—A Fortunate Escape—The Combination of Favorable Circumstances which Resulted in the Saving of Every Soul on Board.

NEW YORK, March 20, 1886.

HAVING procured a state-room in the *Oregon*, of the Cunard line, for myself and my wife, who has been my travelling companion in the journey I have endeavored to describe, we gladly leave the damp and chilly atmosphere of London and spend one night in Liverpool previous to embarking upon the perilous voyage that is to become a notable event in our lives.

We go on board promptly at ten A.M. on Saturday, March 6, anticipating a rapid and safe passage to our home. Leaving Queenstown on Sunday at two P.M., after receiving about six hundred bags of mail which has come from London by rail, we plunge at once into the broad Atlantic to meet, at the very outset, a storm of considerable force. The wonderful speed of the *Oregon* is well illustrated by the fact that she rapidly passed the *Arizona*, which left Queenstown half an hour previously. Having crossed the Atlantic in the *Arizona* on her first voyage East, I well remember that she made the quickest passage that had been accomplished up to that date—seven days, ten hours, and fifty-six minutes from Sandy Hook to Queenstown. Now the *Oregon* has beaten this record by more than a whole day.

As the first part of the passage furnishes little of interest beyond the ordinary routine of events which daily transpire upon an ocean voyage, I propose to devote this letter to a description of the scenes accompanying the loss of the noble steamer that was bearing us so rapidly towards our home.

There seems to have been an unusual anxiety on the part of the Americans aboard to reach their native land. One man, having the appearance of a tiller of the soil, remarked: "I would rather possess one acre of American soil than the whole of the Atlantic Ocean." The week passed rapidly away, and we retired to our state-rooms on Saturday evening, eagerly anticipating the coveted view of our native shore on rising the following morning, little dreaming of the terrible dramatic scenes in which we were about to participate.

As somewhat diverse statements have been given to the public of the scenes that were enacted on board the steamer after the collision, I propose to describe such of these scenes as passed under my own eye with truthful accuracy. In recording the conduct of the officers and crew I shall endeavor to remember the peculiarly trying conditions under which they acted, and to give them all the credit they deserve. At the same time it is due to the passengers of the ill-fated vessel, as well as to the public, that any loss of self-control or dereliction in the performance of their duty should be faithfully noted.

On Sunday morning, March 14, as we were lying in our berths conversing, having been awakened by the noise produced by the hoisting of the mail-bags from the hold, we heard a sudden crash which we thought was produced by the breaking of the steel wire cable, by which the mails were being raised, and the falling upon the deck of the tackle which it sustained. We at once rose and commenced dressing, and in a moment were startled by a loud rap upon the door, and a request to dress ourselves immediately and come on deck as soon as possible. I opened the door suddenly, and the electric light revealed the terror-stricken face of our state-room steward.

By this time all was confusion overhead. The unusual stir and the rushing of hurried footsteps on the deck told us that something serious had happened. The deck was soon crowded with the frightened passengers, but they could find out nothing definite about the accident, and we were all told to go below and finish dressing; that a serious accident had occurred, but that there was no immediate danger. Somewhat reassured, many went below, but it very soon transpired that there had been a collision, and that the steamer was sinking, and by this time she was careened somewhat, which added to the alarm of the passengers.

Up to this moment most of the passengers had only a confused idea that something had happened, as the officers and crew would give no satisfactory answers to their anxious inquiries. But now that they knew the steamer was rapidly sinking, and heard the order given to launch and man the boats, they fully realized their danger.

The scene was most intensely thrilling and

dramatic. Nearly all of the nine hundred people on board were on the main deck, all apparently realizing their extreme peril, and ready to avail themselves of any opportunity which might be presented to escape with their lives. As I witnessed the scene at that moment, and as I look back upon it at this distance, the calmness and self-possession of those people seem wonderful. I refer especially to the cabin passengers, who composed the group immediately around me. Their conduct was such as to enhance one's estimate of human nature.

Nearly all were calm and deliberate, and faced the danger resolutely. The effect produced upon the more excitable natures (of which the writer is a type) was noticeable. The extreme danger had the effect to calm and steady rather than excite these natures. Indeed, among the first cabin passengers there was very little of that boisterous excitement which is supposed to be inspired by such a terrible disaster. There was no loss of self-possession, no frantic shouting, no hysterical praying.

The conduct of the women was admirable. One delicate invalid, who looked so pale and shadowy that it seemed doubtful if she could live to reach her home, seemed inspired with new life by the disaster, and as we met her again on the *Fulda* she was like another being. Her whole frame seemed quivering with fresh vital currents that had flowed into her during these eventful hours.

An elderly woman, who was taken from her husband and transferred to the pilot-boat in one of the first boat-loads, seemed especially calm and self-possessed, and inspired a whole group of women around her with the same feeling. It is said that women are calmer than men in the presence of a great danger, and from what I saw of the bearing of both on this occasion I believe it to be true.

When the first boat-loads of passengers were taken from the steamer to the pilot-boat the officers had pretty good control, and few except women and children were taken; but they soon lost control in a great degree, and the boats, one after another as they came up, were immediately filled with the firemen and more able-bodied and aggressive of the passengers.

The chairman of the board of directors of the Cunard line stated, at a meeting of the stockholders just after the *Oregon* disaster occurred, that the discipline on the steamer was magnificent, and declared that only seven of the firemen jumped into the boats, etc. I was present and saw just what did occur, and am sorry not to agree with him as to the discipline, and my own experience is the best answer to the statement about the firemen. Soon after the first boat-loads left the steamer, which were composed of women and children, the firemen and the more turbulent and muscular of the passengers took possession of each boat and filled it so quickly and with such a rush that I, and others like me, stood no chance whatever, being past the meridian of strength and vigor, and not possessing that kind of aggressiveness required to compete with such elements.

The pilot-boat, which first came upon the scene, was soon filled, mainly with women and children, who were transferred to her by the steamer's boats, and the *Stanley A. Gorham*, a larger schooner, which came up shortly after, was filled in the same manner. During all this time the *Oregon* was gradually sinking, and the situation of those remaining on board of her had become extremely critical. The two schooners had been filled so full that the officers did not dare to receive any more, and all the boats were also filled and floating round. Then no small boats returned for more of the remaining passengers for about an hour. Meantime the water was creeping up the sides of the steamer with ominous rapidity.

There were now about one hundred persons left aboard, the most of whom seemed to me to be passengers. The steamer was settling lower and lower each minute, the prow being considerably lower than the stern, and it seemed that each moment must be the last. We could almost feel the last convulsive quiver preparatory to the final plunge. We all had on life-preservers, and the officers, too, as they walked the bridge at this moment, and for some time previously, had their life-preservers strapped around them, telling the passengers as plainly as possible that the danger was most imminent. Our loved ones had been torn away from us and were floating around in some of the crafts that promised more safety than the doomed steamer, and God only knew whether we should ever meet them again on this side of the dark river. Not a word was spoken. Any unseemly demonstration was impossible, for we were face to face with eternity.

We had to endure this strain for nearly an hour, while no boats were returning to the steamer. Finally we saw two boats approaching in the distance, a large and a small one, and they came up nearly simultaneously. The large one was filled first in almost an instant and rowed away. As the small boat floated past the point where I stood I jumped in, completing the load of eight passengers, which was the limit of her capacity. The revulsion of feeling at this moment was most marked, from the uncertain foothold on the deck of the sinking steamer to the welcome boards of the small boat which had hope in them. As we rowed away we saw other small boats, that had contrived to deposit their loads somewhere, returning to rescue the few passengers remaining on board, and in a few minutes we were taken on board the pilot-boat, where I joined my wife.

After all the passengers and crew had left the steamer, the captain, the doctor, and the carpenter being the very last, and all were contained in the two schooners, which were heavily loaded, and the small boats which were filled, or partially filled, the steamer *Fulda*, of the North German Lloyds line, hove in sight, and, having seen our signals of distress, came promptly to our relief. The feelings of gratitude and joy with which we greeted this good Samaritan of the sea can only be *imagined* by those who were not there to be rescued. Nothing could be more beautiful than her great black hull as she steamed into the midst of that group, composed of the sinking *Oregon*, the two schooners, whose decks were black with people, and the small boats, also filled and floating around within the radius of a mile.

In a few minutes more the noble *Oregon*, which had borne us so swiftly to the very threshold of our homes, gave the final plunge, lifting her stern fifty or sixty feet into the air, and settled into her watery grave. Among the group in which I stood on the deck of the pilot-boat were strong men who turned their backs upon this scene and wept.

The work of transferring to the *Fulda* soon commenced, and in a very short time every one of the nine hundred safely reached her hospitable deck. Here we met with a reception we can never forget. We were literally fed and clothed and housed, for every want was supplied. If we had been brothers and sisters returning from our wanderings after long years of absence we could not have been more lovingly greeted or more tenderly cared for. Although the *Fulda* is much smaller than the *Oregon*, she added nine hundred people to her own crew and passengers, and everything proceeded with the utmost regularity and order. To their credit be it said that the managers of this line would take nothing from the passengers or present any bill to the Cunard line. It was a matter of humanity, not of dollars and cents. I feel—and am sure the *Oregon* passengers all do—that if I ever cross the Atlantic again I shall want to go by the *Fulda*, or at least by some steamer of that line. I should trust myself to the *Fulda* as to an old and valued friend.

One of the most remarkable features of this day's experience was the banishment of the sordid and selfish from all these people. The unselfish and loving spirit that pervaded the *Fulda* was so sensed by the *Oregon* passengers that many men and women wept as they climbed up her sides and met the welcome extended to them. During this whole day, from the moment of the collision until they retired on board the *Fulda* not one of those two hundred cabin passengers showed by word or look that they regretted the loss of their personal effects. Under the inspiration of the terror produced by the imminent danger to which they were exposed, and the gratitude they felt on being rescued, the sordid feeling was held in abeyance for one whole day. This was the most beautiful thing I ever beheld.

But the charm was broken the next morning when the old sordid sphere returned to some of the women sitting opposite to us at the breakfast-table, who were regretting the loss of their diamonds and jewelry, their splendid dresses and beautiful laces which they had bought in Paris. I must say I was ungallant enough to entertain, temporarily, a strong desire to pull their ears. We hope that we shall not live long enough to begin to regret our losses. While the experience is not one we should covet the repetition of, having acquired it, no estimate can be placed upon its value.

The day was filled with incidents of thrilling interest. The impending danger served to develop the best and the worst in those whose lives were imperilled. A venerable judge of the Supreme Court of the United States from a Western State, whose whole face and mien betokened a high type of man, said to a young man standing near, as he was offered a place in a boat about to leave the steamer: "You go; you are a young man with life before you. I am most through." On the other hand, the coal-heavers rushed in and seized the boats, crowding back weaker men, and even women and children.

In one of the boats which was over-crowded, the men threatened to throw overboard some of the passengers, and were only restrained from carrying their threat into execution and inspired with renewed vigor in rowing, by the promise of $500 from a California man if they would put him on the schooner.

The parting of husbands and wives as they were torn asunder when the women left in the first boats, and their meeting again after agonizing hours of separation, was wonderfully exciting and thrilling. Among the group of women on the pilot-boat, as they sat in the cabin awaiting the arrival of their husbands, was a poor little waif of a baby who had got separated from its mother. But the poor little creature received the tenderest care possible till he was restored to the arms of the distracted mother on the *Fulda*.

Many incidents of great interest transpired on the *Fulda*. All hearts were inspired with gratitude, and many embraced and kissed each other in their exuberance of feeling. Indeed, it seemed like one great love-feast.

There seems to be considerable question in

the public mind as to whether the best course was pursued by the officers of the *Oregon* after the collision. Very soon after the accident I distinctly saw the heights on the Long Island shore, but when the vessel sank land was nowhere to be seen. From all I could observe it was quite evident the captain expected that the water-tight compartments would sustain the vessel; and I know he watched very eagerly for some steamer to come and tow her into port. But it seems to me he made a great mistake in not availing himself of all the means in his power to gain a point where he could beach her. (This he well knew meant her destruction.) It seemed as though the momentum and the remaining steam would have enabled him to accomplish this. The chief engineer of the *Oregon* told me in a conversation on the *Fulda*, that when he was forced to leave his post he left the steam on, and that the engine ran two hours from that time, slowing down gradually, so that there was nearly or quite three hours of steaming after the collision. It is claimed that he lost the momentum in turning the vessel round to look for the crew of the colliding schooner; but after all it is a serious question whether he was not too anxious to save the vessel, and so too little regardful of the lives of the passengers. To be sure the precious lives were all saved, but I submit that it was not so much due to the presence of mind and the care and skill of the officers, as to the following favoring conditions:

First—There were eight hours and a quarter between the collision and the sinking.

Second—It was daylight.

Third—The sea was comparatively calm.

Fourth—The pilot-boat came up just in season to receive the first boat-loads of passengers.

Fifth—The schooner *Stanley A. Gorham* appeared upon the scene just at the right moment, after the pilot-boat was filled, to receive a still larger number of passengers.

Sixth—After all the passengers and crew were taken from the *Oregon*, and the two schooners and all the small boats were filled with them—showing most conclusively that the boats of the *Oregon* were entirely insufficient—the *Fulda* hove in sight and steamed into the midst of the group, and took on board every one of the nine hundred who had left the sinking ship.

If any of these favorable conditions had been missing there would have been a terrible loss of life. It is difficult to discover any reason why an earnest attempt should not have been made to beach the vessel, for even in case of failure to accomplish it, we should have been nearer the shore and in shallower water; and if she had been successfully beached there was no reason why the passengers and crew could not have been saved by the small boats and the schooners in exactly the way they were saved further out to sea.

On landing at Hoboken the following morning, the *Oregon* passengers were accorded the first right of way; and a motley-looking procession they were as they filed off in their variegated and miscellaneous garb. They did not experience the least embarrassment in passing their baggage through the hands of the custom-house officers, and soon found themselves in the arms of their anxious friends, who gathered them to their hearts with an especial tenderness.

www.ingramcontent.com/pod-product-compliance
Lightning Source LLC
Chambersburg PA
CBHW022018220426
43663CB00007B/1128